PARENT
POWER

PARENT

POWER

A Program to Help Your Child Succeed in School

SHERRY FERGUSON

LAWRENCE E. MAZIN, Ed.D.

Clarkson N. Potter, Inc./Publishers
DISTRIBUTED BY CROWN PUBLISHERS, INC., NEW YORK

This book is dedicated to all parents who want to assure their children's success in school and life; to all parents who want to be involved with their children's education; to all parents who want to help their children become the best they can be.

Published by Clarkson N. Potter, Inc., 225 Park Avenue South, New York, New York 10003
CLARKSON N. POTTER, POTTER, and colophon are trademarks of Clarkson N. Potter, Inc.

Manufactured in the United States of America

Design by Jan Melchior

Library of Congress Cataloging-in-Publication Data

Ferguson, Sherry, 1948–
Parent power : a program to help your child succeed in school / Sherry Ferguson, Lawrence E. Mazin.
p. cm.
Bibliography: p.
Includes index.
1. Home and school—United States. 2. Education—United States—Parent participation. 3. Parent–teacher relationships—United States. I. Mazin, Lawrence E. II. Title.
LC225.3.F47 1989
370.19'3'0973—dc 19   89-38895
CIP

ISBN 0-517-57107-2
10 9 8 7 6 5 4 3 2 1

First Clarkson N. Potter Edition

ACKNOWLEDGMENTS

Parent Power *began as an idea, a philosophy, and a way of life. We strongly believe that parent involvement is the key to success for our nation's children. This book was written as a result of that conviction and as a part of our crusade to show parents what they need to do to guarantee their children's success in school.*

Many people helped us along the way. First and foremost were our parents, who held high expectations for us. We appreciate the sacrifices they made to assure us every opportunity to be the best we could be. We continue to adhere very strongly to this philosophy for our own children.

We give special thanks to Renee Mazin for providing research for Parent Power *and sincere thanks to both our spouses and children for helping motivate us to write this book.*

Our editor, Jonathan Fox, helped us in a hundred different ways. We thank him for all he has done and for his faith in us. We would also like to thank Nancy Novogrod, whose assistance and confidence in the writing of this book were invaluable.

Our literary agent, Gloria Stern, has been outstanding. She realized and supported our message from the beginning.

Finally, we wish to thank the many students, parents, and educators whose insights and knowledge are reflected in this book.

CONTENTS

INTRODUCTION 1

ONE

PARENTS, STUDENTS, AND SCHOOLS 5

TWO

ACADEMICS PLUS 21

THREE

AFTER-SCHOOL TIME:
HOMEWORK, STUDYING, AND TELEVISION 47

FOUR

SPECIAL PROGRAMS 58

FIVE

MOTIVATING YOUR CHILD TO SUCCEED 70

SIX

SETTING LIMITS: WAYS TO
IMPROVE YOUR CHILD'S BEHAVIOR 95

SEVEN

THE TROUBLED STUDENT 117

EIGHT

THE TIME IT TAKES TO LEARN:
UNDERSTANDING THE SCHOOL DAY 135

NINE

THE FUTURE WITH PARENT POWER 151

NOTES 163

BIBLIOGRAPHY 174

INDEX 180

INTRODUCTION

In the past, "each generation of Americans has outstripped its parents in education, in literacy, and in economic attainment. For the first time in the history of our country, the educational skills of one generation will not surpass, will not equal, will not even approach those of their parents." Why? What is happening in the schools now that has caused this change? What is happening at home? What can parents and teachers do to reverse the trend?

This book is designed to help three groups of people achieve success: educators, parents, and students. As authors, our major goal is to provide you with the basic tools that will assure that your child will learn more, do better in school, and have better opportunities. Along with our major goal, we have identified four other goals:

1. Increasing parent-school communication. We want to unite parents and school in the task of education. Family and school must forge a partnership for the good of the child.
2. Defining the parent's role and responsibilities in a child's education. We seek to reinforce helpful, positive practices, as well as to correct negative attitudes and approaches. Being a responsible parent is hard work, but there are many rewards and joys.
3. Involving other community members in the education process. In order to keep the education system vital, relevant, and successful, the community needs to be aware

of what is happening in our schools and why their support is critical.

4. Letting parents and the community know what is right about education today. In order to keep the education system vital, relevant, and successful, parents and community need to be aware of what is happening in our schools and why their support is critical.

Our book offers plans for positive action. We are not just seeking to present advice. We want to help parents in specific ways: to effectively use early intervention techniques before problems occur; to maintain and build upon good behaviors; and to help their children cope with and change difficult situations. Our solutions, based on experience and common sense, are both practical and successful. That's right: We know they work!

Without the active participation of parents, schools cannot educate America's children. Today, your help is more important than ever because of all the tasks that schools are required to accomplish. At President Reagan's request, the National Commission on Excellence in Education was formed. In April 1983, its findings were compiled in *An Open Letter to the American People: A Nation at Risk: The Imperative for Educational Reform, A Report to the Nation and the Secretary of Education.* The report stated, "School systems in the United States move slowly; even when there is parent pressure for innovations, the changes may come too late to be of benefit to the children now in a particular school, grade or school subject. . . . If the parents wish to improve the learning of their children, the home environment is the only place where they are likely to have some degree of control."

Too often in the past, many educators found it easy to say: "You parents provide the raw material—the children—and we will provide the finished product." This was a superior attitude that told parents: "We are the teaching professionals. We know what your child should be learning and how your child should be learning it. Leave us in charge." This type of posturing had two effects:

1. Society believed the educators. They believed educators were the experts in all areas, and based on this, schools were given more and more tasks to perform. Educators were called upon to step out of their area of expertise. They were expected to succeed in other areas, although they lacked the necessary training.

2. Parents were alienated and antagonized. The very people who should have been the educators' allies began to resent them for assuming a parental role. Some parents believed their authority and values were being questioned or usurped.

Today, this "territorial imperative," establishing strict boundary lines between home and school, is vanishing. Schools realize they need community help, especially if they are to achieve all the tasks that have been given to them.

Although *A Nation at Risk: The Imperative for Educational Reform* covered all phases of education, the main focus was on the school's curriculum, teachers, standards, time-on-task, leadership and fiscal support. These issues are very significant. But most significant are the report's concluding recommendations to parents to ensure their child's success in school:

> **You know you cannot launch your children into today's world unless they are of strong character and well-educated in the use of language, science, and mathematics. They must possess a deep respect for intelligence, achievement, and learning, and the skills needed to use them; for setting goals; and for disciplined work. That respect must be accompanied by an intolerance for the shoddy and second-rate masquerading as "good enough."**
>
> **You have a right to demand for your children the best our schools ... can provide. Your vigilance and your refusal to be satisfied with less than the best are the imperative first step. But your right to a proper education for your children carries a double responsibility ... your child's ideas about education and its significance begin with you. You must be a living example of what you expect your children to honor and to emulate. Moreover, you bear a responsibility to participate actively in your child's education. You should encourage more diligent study and discourage satisfaction with mediocrity and the attitude that says "let it slide"; monitor your child's study; encourage good study habits; encourage your child to take more demanding rather than less demanding courses; nurture your child's curiosity, creativity, and confidence; and be an active participant in the work of the schools. Above all, exhibit a commitment to continue learning in your own life. Finally, help your children understand that excellence in education cannot be achieved without intellectual and moral integrity coupled with hard work and commitment.**

Our book begins where *A Nation at Risk* ends: with the parent—a child's first teacher. In the past, parents have asked, "Can educators provide more 'how to' information that we can use to help our children learn?" Some have even volunteered to pay for these courses themselves—or to pay additional taxes! We want this book to make that unnecessary!

Parent Power shows you the best and most productive ways to help your child succeed in school. We will help you determine how well and how often you contribute to your child's learning and show you hundreds of techniques and active measures you can use to improve the quality of your child's education.

If this book just sits on your bookshelf, then we have accomplished little. It is our greatest hope that it will have well-worn pages, with dog-eared corners, underlinings, and your ideas and comments interjected throughout. Then we will be able to say, "Parent Power . . . it's working!"

PARENTS, STUDENTS, AND SCHOOLS

Parents are the first and most important of their children's educators.

UNIVERSAL DECLARATION OF HUMAN RIGHTS
OF THE UNITED NATIONS CHARTER

The effect that even the best school has on the total education of a child is vastly over-rated and, in comparison with the home . . . relatively small.

NEIL POSTMAN AND CHARLES WIENGARTNER, *THE SCHOOL BOOK*

Your child's education begins with you. You have the right, obligation, and ability to see that your child gets a good education. You can and should make a difference. A child's best teachers are parents who support and encourage learning. The right attitude to education is the most important lesson children can learn. Parents are crucial to this lesson. Parents can make it happen; schools can only reaffirm and build upon that base. Help your child to have a positive attitude toward learning, to learn better, to want to know more, and most of all, to achieve success both in and out of school.

Help your child to develop physically, socially, intellectually, and emotionally.

Through the formative years—until the end of high school—parents nominally control 85 percent of a student's waking time. Their contribution to a child's education is vitally important. What can you do specifically to get your child off to a good start?

- Stimulate your child to use and develop language by talking and reading with him.
- Develop your child's ability to listen by talking with him.
- Encourage your child to develop verbally and artistically by expressing his emotions and exploring his creativity.
- Help your child develop physically by mastering different activities and skills.
- Encourage your child to think, reason, and independently make new discoveries by enriching his environment.
- Motivate your child to find pleasure in learning by engaging him in meaningful activity.
- Encourage your child to develop a sense of mastery over his environment by giving him tasks he can complete.
- Provide opportunities for your child to relate with peers, older and younger people, and people of different backgrounds.
- Develop your child's view of adults as sources of information and ideas, as well as sources of approval and reward.

PARENT ACTION *What You Can Do to Prepare Your Child for School Success* • The following statements describe everyday situations in which you can contribute to your child's learning. Rate yourself on each statement by circling the number that best reflects your support. If you score below a 3 on any item, you need to make some changes in that area.

5	4	3	2	1
ALWAYS	VERY OFTEN	SOMETIMES	RARELY	NEVER

WORK HABITS

1. I stress consistency, sharing, and punctuality in home activities, such as chores.   5 4 3 2 1

2. I emphasize a routine schedule for eating, sleeping, studying, and TV.   5 4 3 2 1

3. I give priority to schoolwork, reading, and other educational activities over TV and recreational activities.   5 4 3 2 1

ACADEMIC GUIDANCE AND SUPPORT

4. I encourage my child in his schoolwork. (This includes giving praise, approval, and rewards, as well as letting others know about his accomplishments.)   5 4 3 2 1

5. I know my child's academic weaknesses and strengths. (This includes learning problems and subject strengths.)   5 4 3 2 1

6. I help or supervise if needed.   5 4 3 2 1

7. I have designated a quiet place in our home (with appropriate reference resources and other learning materials) for my child to study.   5 4 3 2 1

LEARNING STIMULATION

8. My family shares interests in hobbies and games of educational value.   5 4 3 2 1

9. My family reads and discusses books, newspapers, and magazines, as well as TV programs.   5 4 3 2 1

10. Family members freely share opinions.   5 4 3 2 1

11. My family visits libraries and museums and attends other cultural activities.   5 4 3 2 1

LANGUAGE DEVELOPMENT

12. I encourage my family to use correct and effective language.   5 4 3 2 1

13. I encourage my family to increase their vocabulary.   5 4 3 2 1

14. I give my child frequent opportunities to be listened to and to speak.   5 4 3 2 1

PHYSICAL HEALTH

15. I remember to provide lunch or lunch money daily for my child.   5 4 3 2 1

To prepare your young child for school, you should also begin preparing yourself. The following list will help you better understand your child from his perspective.

A CHILD'S TEN COMMANDMENTS TO PARENTS

1. My hands are small; please don't expect perfection when I make a bed, draw a picture, or throw a ball. My legs are short; please slow down so I can keep up.
2. My eyes have not seen the world as yours have; please let me explore safely, don't restrict me unnecessarily.
3. Housework will always be there. I'm only little for such a short time—please take time to explain things to me about this wonderful world, and do so willingly.
4. My feelings are tender: Please be sensitive to my needs; don't nag me all day long. (You wouldn't want to be nagged for your inquisitiveness.) Treat me as you would like to be treated.
5. I am a special gift from God. Please treasure me as God intended you to: holding me accountable for my actions, giving me guidelines to live by, and disciplining me in a loving manner.
6. I need your encouragement to grow. Please go easy on the criticism; remember, you can criticize the things I do without criticizing me.
7. Please give me the freedom to make decisions concerning myself. Permit me to fail, so that I can learn from my mistakes. Then someday I'll be prepared to make the kind of decisions life requires of me.
8. Please don't do things over for me. Somehow that makes me feel that my efforts didn't quite measure up to your expectations. I know it's hard, but please don't try to compare me with my brother or sister.
9. Please don't be afraid to leave for a weekend together. Kids need vacations from parents, too. Besides, it's a great way to show us that your marriage is special.
10. Please give me spiritual guidance. Teach me sound values at home, or take me to religious school and worship; set a good example for me to follow.

16. I make sure my child gets enough sleep by going to bed at an appropriate time on school nights.   5 4 3 2 1

17. I allow time in the morning for breakfast. If necessary, I prepare the table and breakfast foods the night before.   5 4 3 2 1

18. My child attends school properly clothed and groomed for the day's activities.   5 4 3 2 1

19. If my child is ill, I make appropriate arrangements for his care.   5 4 3 2 1

ACADEMIC ASPIRATIONS AND EXPECTATIONS

20. I am familiar with my child's current schoolwork, teachers, texts, progress, and extracurricular activities.   5 4 3 2 1

21. I have and often express high standards and expectations for my child's schoolwork.   5 4 3 2 1

22. I have discussed specific educational and vocational goals with my child.   5 4 3 2 1

23. I help my child make plans to realize educational and vocational goals. (This may include sacrifices of time or money.)   5 4 3 2 1

THE PARENT-TEACHER RELATIONSHIP

"Parents suffer if the teacher-student relationship is bad; teachers suffer if the student-parent relationship is bad. Each has a stake in the relationship that the youngster has with the other adult. Despite this mutual interest in each other's behavior, a parent and teacher seldom have a very close or significant relationship with each other. They don't see each other very often, and when they do, their time together is extremely limited."

One of the reasons parents and teachers have poor relationships stems from the fact that each sees the problems of the schools somewhat differently. Their perceptions of what a school's goals should be may also differ. Here is a comparison from a recent Gallup Poll of what the general public *vs.* educators say are the top ten problems (ranked in order of severity):

PUBLIC	TEACHERS
Lack of discipline	Parent apathy; lack of parent support
Poor curriculum standards	Lack of financial support
Use of drugs	Pupil apathy, truancy
Difficulty in getting good teachers	Lack of discipline
Lack of financial support	Administration problems
Pupil apathy; truancy	Poor curriculum; standards
Large schools; overcrowding	Use of drugs
Integration; busing	Low teacher salaries
Teacher apathy	Difficulty getting good teachers
Drinking; alcoholism	Large schools; overcrowding

In most cases the problems can best be solved not by singling out parents, teachers, or students for blame, but by everyone's working together for success. Some of these issues are not immediately within your grasp to solve and need to be addressed in a larger forum, but strong relationships and good communication between parents and teachers are the best places to start.

If our American educational system is to survive, there must be union among school, family, and community. Teachers and parents working together assure that children believe education to be important. Education for the majority of children will only be successful when there is trust, accountability, and shared responsibility between families, communities, and schools. When teachers and parents work together, children believe education is important.

Accountability is a popular phrase today with those seeking to improve the school system. But accountability works both ways: the school is accountable to parents, but so are the parents accountable to the school. A child's education is a joint effort. Teachers and parents must use each other effectively. Children deserve competent teachers. Good teachers not only teach what to learn, they also teach how to learn it. A qualified teacher should have the following:

- Good human relations skills
- Understanding of learning styles and student development
- An enthusiastic and systematic approach to learning

- Knowledge of the curriculum, texts, and skills to be learned
- Classroom management skills to maintain a good learning environment
- Planning skills
- Ability to use materials creatively

A parent's support of the teacher is as important as his support of his child. A teacher's first line of defense in accomplishing educational goals is the student's parents. The extent of a parent's participation in school responsibilities is often dependent upon a child's stage in school, the parent's expectation levels, financial resources, educational background, commitment to the community, and amount of free time. Each school in this country interacts with adults who can be placed in the following categories. Which category best describes you?

The Task Person. This is the absolute lowest level at which a parent should participate. The task person performs only routine school-related chores; completing forms, writing absentee notes, providing lunch money, signing permission slips and report cards, purchasing appropriate supplies, monitoring homework, dressing the child appropriately, and attending to the child's health (inoculations, physical examinations, nutrition, sleep, and so on). These are obvious tasks any parent should perform, but all too often the school must compensate for parental omission in these areas. This requires additional manpower, which means time and money—all of which are deducted from the academic budget and from the real purpose of school.

The Focused Active Participant. This is the parent who participates in "school life" as long as he has a child attending school. The focused active participant wants to be informed about school activities that affect his child. This parent reads notes and newsletters and calls the school when concerned about his child's progress and welfare. This parent also responds promptly to school queries about these matters. Educators would like all their parents to fall into this category. Active parents improve a child's chance of success in school and support a teacher's efforts.

Active participation includes attending meetings, back-to-school nights, open houses, and conferences. When a parent attends these functions, he should be prepared to do the following:

11

- Exchange information and anecdotes
- Explore and resolve problems
- Examine work, texts, and records
- Learn about curriculum goals and objectives and teaching methods
- Understand the grading system and homework policy
- Meet school personnel in various areas
- Offer and receive suggestions regarding academics, behavior, morale

Focused active participation need not occur only at the invitation of the school. Parents unable to attend meetings can try to reschedule them or call or write to the administrators and teachers. Of course, parents can also call meetings on their own. Parents should always know the key personnel involved in their child's education before a problem arises. Not knowing the teacher could be part of the problem!

Attending athletic and entertainment events is not enough. Sadly, too many parents favor these glamorous activities over direct participation in academic studies. Parents should also reward a child's demonstrations of newly acquired ideas, information, and academic expertise with praise and approval.

Parents must get involved! No one else can take the role of a parent in a child's education. Parental involvement also has an "extra" benefit. By making a meaningful contribution and commitment of themselves through their child, parents can make schools better for all children.

A learning agenda is a good mechanism for getting parents and teachers to work together to help students attain their goals. This is a plan for a child's educational goals during a limited time period. A learning agenda fosters better parent-teacher relationships and understanding. Several agendas could be given to parents during the course of an academic year. Each should be prepared by the teacher and approved by the administration. If none is offered, take the initiative to suggest one to your child's teacher. An agenda should contain the following items:

- Curriculum goals, texts, standards
- Skills to be learned
- Type and quantity of homework to be assigned
- Specific directions showing how parents can help

- Statement of teacher's policy regarding office hours/conferences
- An indication of expectations (both academic and behavioral)

Actually, parents who are intimately involved with their child's education show a greater interest in that child's academic pursuits. In turn, this interest raises expectation levels for their child's performance, which can prove "contagious" to the child. A learning agenda can help parents and teachers work together to create an atmosphere that encourages good study habits, high motivation, and independence—skills that will serve a child throughout his life.

The Nonparticipant. This adult is and will remain childless, has no children in school, or had children who were educated elsewhere. He perceives that he has nothing in common with the community school district. If concerned about schools at all, he desires that they be "good" from a neighborhood viewpoint; that is, they should keep the community safe, keep property values high and stable, and attract industries and businesses to his town. In all likelihood he has not been in a school since his own or his last child's graduation. Often this adult can be quite vocal when tax issues are raised. It is critical for schools and parents alike to try to "move" this type of individual into the category of active observer.

The Active Observer. This adult is childless or does not have a child presently enrolled in the school. Unlike the nonparticipant, the active observer attends school events because of a commitment to community or to education. These events usually have entertainment or athletic value. This type of participation is becoming more critical to school personnel, parents, and students because of a lower birth rate and an aging population.

The active observer believes that educating children is the responsibility of everyone. Each educational dollar invested is returned tenfold, and educated children give all citizens their money's worth. Today's young people are tomorrow's foundation for progress, inventions, services, and the economy. They should be given the same opportunity afforded others who have graduated, found success, and contributed to society. Why should someone become an active observer? Because everyone benefits in some way:

• School support is important to maintain the American way of life.

". . . paying for education is an investment in ever-renewable human resources that are more durable and flexible than capital plant and equipment . . ."

• Everyone "owns" the schools and everyone is responsible for them, regardless of age or parental status.

"What goes on in local schools affects virtually everything else that we do as a nation, which is the main reason why school taxes are levied on every member of the community."

• One out of four dollars in the federal budget goes to a senior citizen from income generated by a younger worker. Information and equipment developed by younger workers extends and makes more comfortable the lives of many seniors. These advances are made possible by research and education—which began in the public schools. For these reasons, senior citizens should be active observers and education's strongest supporters.

To increase active observer support, schools should offer outreach programs and the use of their facilities, such as cafeterias, auditoriums, gymnasiums, meeting rooms, and classrooms. Schools should publicize and place greater emphasis on academic nights, job/career fairs, adult education, skill-building workshops, and seminars to attract adults, and should involve them in the welfare of the school. People become active observers when schools meet their needs. In turn, every member of the community benefits. Being an active observer is the first step toward becoming a volunteer.

The Volunteer. This adult provides real support for the teacher. He has the time, energy, the financial ability, or the expertise to participate regularly in the community schools in one of the following capacities, with little compensation:

• Crossing guard
• Grandparent program

- Coach assistant
- Classroom monitor
- Teachers' aide
- Sharer of interests/hobbies/talents
- Fund raiser
- Class trip monitor

A special and prominent category of volunteers is the Parent Teacher Association (PTA) or Parent Teacher Organization (PTO). Their memberships have become increasingly more involved in linking the home and school. The kinds of activities and degrees of activism of these organizations may vary from school to school, but they are never "for women only." Members might be involved in public relations, communications, fund-raising, sponsoring pilot programs, lobbying the legislature for a change in the law or increased funds, maintaining a dialogue with teachers and administrators, developing parent centers and programs, and staging special school events.

Schools need more volunteers, better programs for recruiting volunteers, funds to organize and develop volunteer programs, and better ways to use the talents of people willing to share them.

The Policymaker. This adult serves the school and its interests from a position of power—as a school board member. The United States has about 15,000 school districts with 100,000 school board members overseeing a total of 80,000 schools. Each school district usually has its own school board. Most school board members are lay people, not professional educators. The expertise they bring to school administration comes from many fields, which can be both positive and negative.

Ideally, a school board member should be either a focused active participant, an active observer, or a volunteer. However, a nonparticipant or task person may also successfully seek this role, often to the detriment of the school district. These are the few who are useless, adversarial, meddling, or ineffective.

The powers and functions of school boards vary by district, but they may include:

- Setting educational policies, standards, and guidelines; developing curriculum; and selecting texts.

- Serving as a public forum and linking the school to the community.
- Planning, building, and remodeling facilities.
- Drafting budgets, issuing bonds, overseeing capital investments.
- Entering into contracts with school personnel and outside agencies providing goods and services for the school district.
- Evaluating, hiring, and dismissing all school district personnel.
- Managing school real estate and facilities.
- Acting as a community's largest employer (as the school board is in many regions).
- Overseeing the operation of a transportation system, cafeteria service, data processing center.
- Handling large volume purchasing of school supplies, textbooks, equipment, and other materials.
- Handling health and liability insurance for staff and students.
- Handling public relations and disseminating information about district events and policies.
- Promoting training and development for teachers, administrators, and support staff.
- Adjudicating student discipline cases.

Considering that the economic strength of school boards totals more than $159.3 billion, it is remarkable that school board elections have low voter turnout. One-third of all school board members either run unopposed or are appointed. A Gallup Poll reported that 53 percent of adults did not know the names of their school board members. It is not necessary for every adult (or parent) to seek a seat on the school board, but all members of the community should be familiar with school board members and school issues. These, too, affect their children's education.

Private school boards may not have all the legal powers given to public school boards. Those who serve are generally not elected by the community that pays for that school's services, but may be appointed by the school or its other board members because of financial prominence or professional expertise.

All private school boards differ from public school boards in that they have no legal authority for bonding or taxing. They do not have any formal link with government offices involved with overseeing aspects of school compliance (these can include the county attorney and the state legislature). In turn, state education control agencies and the legislature have minimal impact on private school boards. For example, private schools can select their students. They are not required to educate or provide facilities for handicapped students. These are tasks that public schools are mandated to perform.

The Professionals. These are the school staff and administrators (and some parents) who may be representative of the larger community they serve in terms of their abilities, interests, and religious or ethnic backgrounds. Besides representing the community in these ways, they also form their own community. The best "school" communities have the following characteristics:

- An administrator who is a staff leader, program designer, and coordinator adept at community relations.
- Teachers who are professional in their educational techniques. These teachers have high expectations for all their students.
- A strong focus on the basic skills such as math and reading.
- An orderly school climate.
- An evaluation system for students that is used frequently and consistently.

Community members and parents might measure their school in these areas to determine where improvements should be made. Above all, increased parental involvement is most important to a child's education.

PARENTS' RIGHTS

Parents and students both have rights that are an integral part of accountability. These rights ensure you a voice in shaping your child's education and also ensure you the necessary information to make informed and intelligent decisions. As a parent you have the right to an active role with input and feedback.

Parents (and other adults) have the right to be heard and to discuss problems involving their children and the schools. Even in ideal situations, problems arise; differences of opinion occur. Schools are aware of this and want your input. Educators do not want parents to sit back and let the school do it all, especially when there is a problem. Even if there is a disagreement, good teachers will not take it out on your kids. In fact, they will probably be grateful that you are concerned enough to disagree. Be part of the educational process for your child's sake. Your parental rights come with parental responsibilities. You should:

- **Monitor your child's progress.**
- **Review instructional material.**
- **Visit the school and meet the people involved in your child's education. Too often schools have an "Open House" that only 10 percent of the parents attend.**
- **Review school policies, research, and planning reports.**
- **Attend school board meetings.**
- **Make demands. If you want more science, math, and computer technology, let the school board know. Then support these educational programs with money at budget time.**

You can also request the information that follows:

Evaluation. Schools should tell you how your child is evaluated, placed, and promoted. These procedures vary from school to school. Evaluation, placement, and promotion have social as well as academic implications. Any positive or negative action regarding these decisions is generally more beneficial if done early in your child's educational career. Schools will discuss the criteria, standards, and input used to make these decisions. School personnel will inform you of alternatives and make the best recommendation for your child, based on their expertise, appraisals, and experience.

School Records. You have the right to examine your child's school records in order to get a complete picture of him as a student and the education he receives. These records may include:

• Attendance records
• Evaluations/grades
• Guidance records
• Health records
• Enrollment records
• Special services records
• Disciplinary action reports
• Test records

Parental access to records is guaranteed by the Freedom of Information Act (Buckley Amendment, 1974 Family Educational Rights and Privacy Act). The act also prohibits release of student records to other agencies or individuals without permission. It allows records to be challenged if parents believe they are inaccurate or misleading. This can be done formally or informally. In a formal setting, parents are given a hearing to voice and prove their viewpoint. This is called due process.

Due process should not be necessary if parents and educators act receptively, responsibly, and respectfully toward each other throughout the child's student years. You need to play an active part in your child's education from the very beginning.

Due process for special education students requires the following:

1. Notice is given concerning the time and place for a due process hearing.
2. All pertinent school records are made available for review by parents.
3. Parents may request an independent evaluation and review of school records.
4. Both parents and school are entitled to counsel, cross-examination, witnesses, and evidence at the due process hearing.
5. Both parents and the school receive records of the proceedings.

The common goal for both the parent and the school is a resolution in the best interests of the child. Keeping the lines of communication open between parent and teacher should avoid any other outcome and should limit the need for such actions.

STUDENTS' RIGHTS

As a parent you must be acquainted with your child's rights as a student. If your child's rights are being violated, then indeed so are yours. Basic rights given students include the following:

- A free, appropriate, and equal education.
- Freedom of speech and assembly.
- Freedom to publish, distribute, and possess literature.
- Limited freedom-under-search procedures. The Supreme Court ruled in January, 1985, that educators can examine a student's belongings without a search warrant. Educators can search book bags, lockers, purses, and gym bags for drugs, alcohol, and weapons. The most significant part of this ruling is that it implied that students do not have the same rights as adults in a school situation.
- The right to appeal suspension or severe discipline.
- The right to appeal for a different classroom designation.
- Participation in extracurricular activities, regardless of sex, physical handicap, etc.
- Permission to be excused from reading certain books (or from participating in certain activities) on religious or moral grounds.

TWO

ACADEMICS PLUS

The school curriculum is a plan of subjects and skills to be learned. It includes basic academic skills, some course work that is mandated by state law, and courses offered by the individual school. Since the subjects that can be offered depend upon a school district's financial ability to develop courses and to attract qualified staff, strong community interest and support are necessary. Not all courses of study receive the same funding: For instance, most school districts currently allocate more money for basic programs and "life-skill" courses than for the arts. Allocation is often the result of educational trends and public pressure, not educational research, which is another reason active participation on your part is important.

Know your child's curriculum so you can help him learn. Helping him requires time and commitment and—most of all—high expectations, if results are to be successful.

Beginning with the basics, this chapter lists the subjects taught in most schools. The skills needed for each subject have been noted to give you a clearer understanding of your child's educational goals and objectives in that course.

Schools teach better with even minimal educational reinforcement from parents. Share your child's learning experiences. Under Parent Action is a checklist of everyday situations in which you can help your child succeed in learning.

21

READING

Reading is a critical area of learning. It is one of the keys to good communication, and is vital to career development. It is also the link to all other subject areas. Reading is required in 80 percent of all classwork. One study of a group of fifth graders (from *Becoming a Nation of Readers*) found the following after-school reading patterns in children:

- 50 percent read four minutes per day.
- 30 percent read two minutes or less per day.
- 10 percent did not read at all.

In this Westernized and technologically advanced civilization, it has been estimated that 21.7 percent of adults ages 17 to 65 (23 million) cannot complete applications or read want ads, medicine labels, or safety signs.

The competent reader can:

- Comprehend the main idea and details.
- Make inferences.
- Summarize ideas in his own words and draw conclusions.
- Understand point of view, recognize the difference between fact and opinion, and understand motives of characters.
- Vary reading speed and method according to task.
- Understand the parts and purposes of a book.
- Understand different types of writing, including biography, poetry, nonfiction, fiction, and journalism.
- Appreciate the American literary heritage and the values and morals that literature illustrates and transmits.
- Use literature to gain insight into the human condition and to understand how people behave.
- Gain enjoyment and inspiration from reading.

PARENT ACTION *What You Can Do to Help Your Child Succeed in Reading* • The following statements describe everyday situations in which you can contribute to your child's reading ability. Rate yourself on each statement by circling the number that best reflects your support. If you score below a 3 on any item, make some changes in that area.

5	4	3	2	1
ALWAYS	VERY OFTEN	SOMETIMES	RARELY	NEVER

1. I encourage my child to read by rewarding and praising his reading efforts.   5 4 3 2 1

2. I discuss with my child what he is reading in school and at home.   5 4 3 2 1

3. My child reads aloud to family members.   5 4 3 2 1

4. I help my child isolate difficult words or sentences, then read for meaning.   5 4 3 2 1

5. I encourage my child to use a dictionary, almanac, atlas, thesaurus, encyclopedia, and telephone directory.   5 4 3 2 1

6. I use my child's teacher as a resource person. *Learn about reading methods, tasks, and exercises you can do at home. Request additional reading material for school assignments to supplement textbooks.*   5 4 3 2 1

7. I use car trips and travel time with my child for reading road signs, following a map, and playing word games.   5 4 3 2 1

8. I play word games with my child. *Games can build vocabulary, explore multiple meanings, and teach idioms.*   5 4 3 2 1

9. My child and I visit the library and attend library programs.   5 4 3 2 1

10. We have books, newspapers, and magazines in our home. *Purchase them with your child and build a home library. Choose material that is interesting and challenging.*   5 4 3 2 1

11. I read for enjoyment. *Children learn by imitation. Your enjoyment of reading shows that it is a rewarding and worthwhile activity.*   5 4 3 2 1

12. I read aloud to my child. *Reading aloud should not diminish as your child grows. Reading aloud is for all members of the*   5 4 3 2 1

family, not just Mother and not just at bedtime. Do not make it a chore. Enjoy reading. Choose books with interesting plots,
good characterizations and dialogue. Set
the mood, pause to build suspense, and re-
capitulate. Encourage discussion, expression, and reaction.

WRITING

*Writing holds us responsible for our words . . . in reading every-
thing is provided, [but] . . . in writing, the learner must supply everything.*

Writing is basic and fundamental to communication. The best
and brightest ideas, if not properly expressed, remain trapped in a
student's mind. Writing skills are declining. The written word has
competition from telephones, greeting cards (which substitute for
writing and thinking our own thoughts), and the attitude that writing skills are unnecessary for successful employment. Increasingly,
it is said, adults do not write anything more than shopping lists.

The competent writer can:

- Organize ideas.
- Write in standard English, using correct sentence struc-
  ture, verb tenses, punctuation, capitalization, possessives,
  plurals, and spelling.
- Use appropriate vocabulary for his grade level or assign-
  ment.
- Edit and rewrite correctly.
- Use research materials properly.
- Develop good handwriting and typing skills. (The latter is
  also a useful computer skill.)

PARENT
ACTION
*What You Can Do to Help Your Child Succeed in Writ-
ing* • The following statements describe everyday situations in which you can contribute to your child's
writing ability. Rate yourself on each statement by circling the
number that best reflects your support. If you score below a 3 on
any item, make some changes in that area.

5	4	3	2	1
ALWAYS	VERY OFTEN	SOMETIMES	RARELY	NEVER

1. In the past week, my child has seen me write more than a grocery list or a check. *Children learn by example.*   5 4 3 2 1

2. I share with my child letters that I've received at home or at work.   5 4 3 2 1

3. I encourage my child to improve penmanship by developing good eye/hand coordination in drawing and other handicrafts.   5 4 3 2 1

4. I encourage my child to write and design thank-you notes and birthday cards.   5 4 3 2 1

5. My child helps to keep a family journal or scrapbook of important events.   5 4 3 2 1

6. All members of my family try to use correct grammar.   5 4 3 2 1

7. I encourage my child to read his finished written projects aloud to the family.   5 4 3 2 1

8. I discuss with my child his school writing assignments.   5 4 3 2 1

9. I encourage my child to participate in writing-oriented clubs or electives, such as the school newspaper.   5 4 3 2 1

10. I dictate short lists or notes. *This works especially well with younger children.*   5 4 3 2 1

11. I make certain that my child has a variety of writing materials; personalized stationery, notepaper, attractive pencils or pens, address books, diaries, daily planners, assignment pads, and calendars.   5 4 3 2 1

SPEAKING AND LISTENING SKILLS

"In our verbal culture we speak much more than we write. We use the telephone more frequently than we send letters. Talk is everywhere. Throughout our lives we judge others, and we ourselves are judged by what is said . . . [students] should be taught to evaluate what they hear, to understand how ideas can be clarified or distorted, and to explore how the accuracy and reliability of an oral message can be tested."

"Research has shown that the average 12-year-old communicates with his or her parents for only fourteen and a half minutes per day. Of this interval, the child spends twelve and a half minutes receiving reprimands, discipline and criticism."

Another recent survey cited that parents "talk seriously" to their children less than three minutes per week. Parents experience different stages of communication with their children. When a child is an infant, parents cannot wait for him to say his first word. Later, when their toddler talks constantly, mimicking every spoken word, parents want a reprieve from the constant chatter. When that same child becomes an adolescent, parents say, "I can't talk to my child" or "I can't get my child to talk to me."

No matter how old your child is now, you can and should communicate with him. Communication is important for your child because it:

- Shows your love, care, and concern.
- Develops self-worth in your child and builds confidence.
- Builds creativity and imagination.
- Helps your child define his identity.
- Encourages self-expression.
- Develops good speech habits and patterns.
- Exposes your child to different ideas and opinions.
- Encourages critical thinking.
- Helps your child avoid behavior problems.

The competent speaker and listener can:

- Understand what is being said, and ask questions if he does not.
- Exchange ideas clearly.
- Use appropriate language.
- Follow instructions.
- Organize a presentation.
- Evaluate presentations.
- Participate in group discussions, debates, and reading aloud.

<u>**PARENT**</u>
<u>*ACTION*</u> *What You Can Do to Help Your Child Succeed in Speaking and Listening Skills* • The following statements describe everyday situations in which you can contribute to your child's ability to speak and listen well. Rate yourself on each statement by circling the number that best reflects your support. If you score below a 3 on any item, make some changes in that area.

5	4	3	2	1
ALWAYS	VERY OFTEN	SOMETIMES	RARELY	NEVER

1. I take time to listen to and speak with my child.   5 4 3 2 1

2. I play games with my child that require careful listening, rhyming, directions, and repetition.   5 4 3 2 1

3. I encourage my child to speak by listening respectfully to his ideas and suggestions and by giving him a "full hearing."   5 4 3 2 1

4. I encourage the expressive use of language. *Set an example by varying your pace, tone, and inflection.*   5 4 3 2 1

5. I stress the importance of proper speech and pronunciation.   5 4 3 2 1

6. If my child has a speech problem, such as poor articulation or stuttering, I allow him to express ideas without fear of constant correction, ridicule, criticism, or rejection.   5 4 3 2 1

7. I encourage my child to listen to appropriate radio shows.   5 4 3 2 1

8. If I am bilingual, I stress the importance of learning the language of the dominant culture. *This can be done while maintaining your heritage, culture, and language.*   5 4 3 2 1

MATHEMATICS

In helping a child develop math skills, schools are ensuring that he will have a basic tool with which to approach numerous everyday situations throughout his life.

The competent math student can:

- Perform basic skills of addition, subtraction, division, and multiplication.
- Use natural numbers, fractions, decimals, and integers.
- Use and understand measurements, ratios, proportions, percentages, roots, powers, algebra, graphs, geometry, probablility, and statistics.
- Be able to make estimates and approximations. Know if results are reasonable.
- Apply math skills to common situations such as shopping or managing a savings account.
- Resolve math problems using appropriate tools and methods.

PARENT ACTION *What You Can Do to Help Your Child Develop Mathematics Skills* • The following statements describe everyday situations in which you can contribute to your child's math ability. Rate yourself on each item by circling the number that best reflects your support. If you score below a 3 on any item, make some changes in that area.

5	4	3	2	1
ALWAYS	VERY OFTEN	SOMETIMES	RARELY	NEVER

1. I use grocery trips to teach math to my child. *Point out costs and weights of items. Compare brands and prices. Show your child how to maximize a budget by taking advantage of coupons, "specials," sales, and store brands. Let your child pay the cashier and count up the change.*   5 4 3 2 1

2. My child and I perform tasks and play games requiring math skills, such as sorting, comparing, perceiving patterns, memorizing, sequencing, estimating, and recognizing shapes.   5 4 3 2 1

3. I discuss measurement concepts with my child; how to tell time; timing the cooking of food, exercise, athletic events.   5 4 3 2 1

4. I indicate the importance of following pre-   5 4 3 2 1

cise mathematical instructions when cook-   5   4   3   2   1
ing, measuring, doing woodworking proj-
ects, or reading maps.

5. My child has access to a small calculator   5   4   3   2   1
and understands how to use it.

6. I give my child—if old enough—responsi-   5   4   3   2   1
bility to purchase groceries, his own items of
clothing, and supplies.

SCIENCE

An education in science prepares students to understand and
evaluate such issues as nuclear power, genetic engineering, pollu-
tion control, conservation, energy, information processing, and
organ transplants. In the future, many high-paying jobs will be in
these technological areas.

The competent science student can:

- Understand the role of science in daily life.
- Understand social and environmental implications of science and technology.
- Understand laboratory work and methods.
- Understand fundamental relationships, laws, concepts,
  and processes of discovery.
- Participate successfully in science course work, including
  biology, earth science, environmental science, chemistry,
  and physics.

PARENT ACTION *What You Can Do to Help Your Child Succeed in Science*
• The following statements describe everyday situa-
tions in which you can contribute to your child's science ability. Rate yourself on each item by circling the number that
best reflects your support. If you score below a 3 on any item, make
some changes in that area.

5	4	3	2	1
ALWAYS	VERY OFTEN	SOMETIMES	RARELY	NEVER

1. I explain the reason for health check-ups   5   4   3   2   1
and visits to the dentist and doctor.

2. I offer my child an opportunity to learn   5   4   3   2   1

about animals and plants by visiting zoos
and parks or caring for a pet.

3. I discuss nutrition and food additives. *Use*   5 4 3 2 1
   your kitchen as a "lab."

4. I discuss the life cycle, the human body,   5 4 3 2 1
   sexual development, and reproduction.

5. I discuss today's technology with my child.   5 4 3 2 1
   This includes the cost and efficiency of en-
   ergy sources; computer-based industries, in-
   formation, and occupations.

6. I discuss the use of chemicals in cleaners,   5 4 3 2 1
   lawn products, and other materials we frequently use.

7. I allow my child to operate equipment   5 4 3 2 1
   such as cameras, calculators, and com-
   puters.

8. I encourage participation in community   5 4 3 2 1
   science fairs and competitions.

9. I supplement the information in my child's   5 4 3 2 1
   school science texts with current pe-
   riodicals.

10. I encourage hobbies, the use of science   5 4 3 2 1
    kits, and outdoor experiences such as
    camping and hiking.

COMPUTERS

Computer technology has implications for jobs and for the
learning process. Future educational uses of computers in schools
include programmed learning for basic skills, tutoring, self-paced
instruction, self-testing, simulation, game playing, guidance,
drills, and practice. Using computers for drills and practice will
give teachers time for more individualized instruction. The successful adaptation of computers in schools is dependent upon cost,
personnel training, and expertise, availability of programs, and
daily hands-on use by teachers themselves. Computers can also be
linked with resource and data bases, libraries, universities, and
museums, so that there can be greater access to information in the
school and in the home. Home-based learning may change the
length of the school day, as well as the structure of schools as they
exist today.

The competent student using computers can:

- Understand computer terminology.
- Know how computers work and process information.
- Evaluate and understand software.
- Know where and how computers are used.
- Understand how computers are used for communication, computation, and information retrieval.

PARENT ACTION *What You Can Do to Increase Your Child's Computer Literacy* • The following statements describe everyday situations in which you can contribute to your child's ability to use computers. Rate yourself on each item by circling the number that best reflects your support. If you score below a 3 on any item, make some changes in that area.

5	4	3	2	1
ALWAYS	VERY OFTEN	SOMETIMES	RARELY	NEVER

1. I know how computers are used in my child's education. *Is your child learning about the computer, using it for other course work, and using it to access information? All these abilities are required for computer literacy.*
   5 4 3 2 1

2. I know the quality and purpose of the software my child uses. *If possible, give your child access to a small computer.*
   5 4 3 2 1

3. I discuss how computers are used in my workplace for check processing or information storage and retrieval.
   5 4 3 2 1

4. I explain how computers and other machines we use daily save time and money. These include computerized library card catalogs, automatic tellers, and lasers that read bar codes in the supermarkets.
   5 4 3 2 1

5. I explain how computers and other technologies affect the quality of life. My child and I discuss the positive and negative aspects of these changes.
   5 4 3 2 1

SOCIAL STUDIES

Social studies includes history, government, economics, civics, sociology, geography, and anthropology. These subjects are important for maintaining democracy and building an informed electorate. Social studies helps children learn about the world around them, as well as to learn about how other cultures have different customs, traditions, and beliefs. In order to deal with the future successfully, children need to know about the past. In most states, it is necessary to complete courses about that state's history, as well as United States history and the Constitution.

The competent student of social sciences can:

- Know geography.
- Understand his culture's link with the past and possibilities for the future.
- Examine contemporary trends.
- Know the history of social and cultural developments.
- Understand the relationship and history of the United States and other countries.
- Understand the processes and functions of American political and economic institutions.
- Know the differences between free and repressive societies.

PARENT ACTION *What You Can Do to Help Your Child in Social Studies•* The following statements describe everyday situations in which you can increase your child's ability in the social sciences. Rate yourself on each item by circling the number that best reflects your support. If you score below a 3 on any item, make some changes in that area.

5	4	3	2	1
ALWAYS	VERY OFTEN	SOMETIMES	RARELY	NEVER

1. My child and I discuss current events described in newspapers and other media. 5 4 3 2 1

2. My child and I consider the impact of current events on our community and family. 5 4 3 2 1

3. I show my child how current events influence developments in art, literature, and music. 5 4 3 2 1

4. I visit historical sites and museums with my child. 5 4 3 2 1

5. I link my "family history" with events of the past. *Let your child know how your family has been affected by history, or how it has participated in politics.* 5 4 3 2 1

6. I encourage my child to write to government representatives about appropriate issues that may concern him. 5 4 3 2 1

7. My child and I play games to develop skills in geography. 5 4 3 2 1

8. As a family, we attend fairs, exhibits, or celebrations to gain greater awareness of different cultural groups. 5 4 3 2 1

FOREIGN LANGUAGES

Proficiency in a language usually requires four to six years of study—more time than is allowed by most school districts. For that reason, such study should begin in elementary school, rather than in the junior or senior high school years.

The competent foreign language student can:

- Converse, pronounce, read, and write in a foreign language.
- Become more sensitive to the traditions of other cultures.
- Develop greater appreciation of the literature, music, and art of other cultures.
- More fully enjoy travel in other countries.
- Recognize language proficiency as a link to international commerce, diplomacy, and shared cross-cultural knowledge.

PARENT
ACTION

What You Can Do to Help Your Child Learn Languages
• The following statements describe everyday situations in which you can contribute to your child's foreign language ability. Rate yourself on each item by circling the number that best reflects your support. If you score below a 3 on any item, make some changes in that area.

• • •

5	4	3	2	1
ALWAYS	VERY OFTEN	SOMETIMES	RARELY	NEVER

1. I share my family's heritage with my child.   5   4   3   2   1
2. My family expresses interest in other cultures.   5   4   3   2   1
3. I describe achievements of other cultures to my child.   5   4   3   2   1
4. I expose my child to foreign language recordings, films, books, and magazines.   5   4   3   2   1
5. I indicate the many ways in which knowing a second language can be beneficial to my child.   5   4   3   2   1
6. When possible, I give my child the opportunity to experience different cultures by traveling, tasting foreign cuisines, and attending events reflecting other cultures.   5   4   3   2   1

THE ARTS: DANCE, DRAMA, MUSIC, AND VISUAL ARTS

A child's appreciation and enjoyment of the arts allows for increased self-awareness, expression, creativity, understanding, and a more complete interpretation of the world around him. Many courses in the arts are designed to help the student develop a historical perspective and appreciation, as well as encourage active participation in various arts.

The competent student of the arts can:

- Understand and appreciate different media, cultures, historical periods, social influences, skills, tools, and artistic processes.
- Evaluate and critique artistic endeavors.
- Enjoy and express himself through artistic pursuits.
- Recognize the role of the arts in our heritage, in communication, and self-expression.
- Gain confidence to use his imagination to express himself.
- Learn self-discipline by pursuing the development of skills to perfect his ability and knowledge in one or more of the arts.

PARENT ACTION *What You Can Do to Help Your Child Enjoy the Arts •* The following statements describe everyday situations in which you can contribute to your child's artistic interests. Rate yourself on each item by circling the number that best reflects your support. If you score below a 3 on any item, make some changes in that area.

5	4	3	2	1
ALWAYS	VERY OFTEN	SOMETIMES	RARELY	NEVER

1. I support my child's artistic efforts with opportunities to develop his skills.   5 4 3 2 1

2. I recognize and support my child's artistic interests even if he does not show talent in the arts. Other benefits my child gains through art appreciation are relaxation, reduction of stress, satisfaction of creating, and a sense of appreciation for somebody else's efforts.   5 4 3 2 1

3. My child and I attend concerts, shows, operas, dance recitals, musicals, art fairs, and visit museums, and I discuss these visits with my child.   5 4 3 2 1

4. I enjoy art—such as paintings and music— in my home.   5 4 3 2 1

5. If I am involved in dance, drawing, music, crafts, or dramatic projects, I encourage my child's active participation.   5 4 3 2 1

6. I help my child relate his efforts to other areas. *An aspiring musician might also want to learn techniques of record production. There are many occupations related to the theater besides acting, such as set design or publicity.*   5 4 3 2 1

PHYSICAL EDUCATION

Physical education may include teaching good health habits, nutrition, exercise, and the development of team or individual sports. The child who feels comfortable with his body and who masters physical skills has a healthier self-image. He finds satisfaction in the development of his skills and athletic accomplishments, both individually and as part of a team.

The competent student of physical education can:

- Increase physical stamina, coordination, balance, dexterity, strength, flexibility, and control.
- Learn the value of competitive sports and the team experience.
- Use athletic participation as an emotional outlet to promote a sense of well-being and relaxation.
- Develop a desire to participate in athletics, either as part of a team or individually, after the school years.

PARENT ACTION *What You Can Do to Help Your Child in Physical Education* • The following statements describe everyday situations in which you can contribute to your child's physical skills. Rate yourself on each item by circling the number that best reflects your support. If you score below a 3 on any item, make some changes in that area.

5	4	3	2	1
ALWAYS	VERY OFTEN	SOMETIMES	RARELY	NEVER

1. I am teaching my young child basic body movements: how to hop, skip, jump, slide, tiptoe, stamp, whirl, run, gallop, leap, prance, crawl, and kick.   5 4 3 2 1

2. I encourage my child to dance and move to music.   5 4 3 2 1

3. I show my child how to do basic exercises.   5 4 3 2 1

4. I share my interest in sports and athletics with my child by participating in athletics and attending sporting events.   5 4 3 2 1

5. I attend school athletic events in which my child participates.   5 4 3 2 1

6. Together my child and I attend and enjoy other school athletic events.   5 4 3 2 1

7. If possible, I encourage my child to partici-   5 4 3 2 1

pate in athletics by belonging to a gym or   5   4   3   2   1
club that provides facilities and programs
for young people.

8. By my own example, I encourage my child   5   4   3   2   1
to exercise regularly, develop healthy eat-
ing habits, and maintain a sensible sleeping schedule.

9. I respect my child's physical efforts and   5   4   3   2   1
limits.

10. I let my child choose the activities in which   5   4   3   2   1
he wants to participate. Without pushing
him, I support his best efforts in those activities.

HOME ECONOMICS AND INDUSTRIAL ARTS

Traditionally, home economics was for girls and industrial arts for boys. In the past, parents also taught these skills to their children through activities such as needlework, cooking, woodworking, and agriculture. They were taught explicitly because some task needed to be done or implicitly by example. Today, as required by law, schools offer electives in home economics and industrial arts to both sexes. Skills learned in both areas can provide a sense of competency and satisfaction to the student. At home, parents should do tasks based on ability and interest, not on traditional sex roles.

The competent student in each of these areas can:

- Understand all facets of home economics including consumerism, nutrition, sewing and clothes design, interior decoration, maintaining and developing good health, caring for young children, and developing interpersonal skills within the family.
- Master industrial arts, including working with a variety of tools and materials. These often include an introduction to design and building in the areas of woodworking and metalworking. Students also learn how to properly care for, organize, and maintain tools and equipment.

• • •

PARENT ACTION — *What You Can Do to Help Your Child Develop Skills in Home Economics and Industrial Arts* • The following statements describe everyday situations in which you can contribute to your child's abilities in these areas. Rate yourself on each item by circling the number that best reflects your support. If you score below a 3 on any item, make some changes in that area.

5	4	3	2	1
ALWAYS	VERY OFTEN	SOMETIMES	RARELY	NEVER

1. I include my child in the running of our household by assigning him appropriate chores. 5 4 3 2 1

2. I openly discuss aspects of family life, such as health, nutrition, and meal planning. 5 4 3 2 1

3. When working on a household project, I discuss the process with my child and request his assistance, if possible. 5 4 3 2 1

4. I assign tasks to my child based on ability, need, and interest, instead of traditional sex roles. 5 4 3 2 1

5. When building projects or making repairs, I involve my child. This may include shopping for materials, taking measurements, and explaining instructions. 5 4 3 2 1

6. When planning a meal or a party, I involve my child in the purchase and preparation of food. 5 4 3 2 1

VOCATIONAL/CAREER/CO-OP EDUCATION

"Expenditures authorized by the VEA (Vocational Education Act) are by far the largest federal contribution to secondary schools."

Vocational course work is becoming increasingly popular. Course emphasis is on neither theory nor academics, but rather on developing practical skills designed to help a student function in the "real world of work." Advocates state that these classes:

- *"Meet the needs of 85 percent of the persons who enter and work in the nation's work force."* These are the people who find work in fields that do not require a college education.

- Mainstream the disadvantaged into the work force. In the past, and unfortunately to some degree today, these courses were thought to be best suited to minorities and immigrants.
- Serve as a realistic training center for those who will not pursue higher education.
- Teach skills that are needed in the job areas where demand is the highest. Some current examples of these areas include computer repair and service, robotics, and secretarial work.
- Keep in school those most likely to fall into the traps of juvenile crime, gangs, or teenage pregnancy.

Critics of vocational education are concerned about the serious problems that exist in many vocational programs. Here are ten issues to consider before your child enrolls in vocational classes. Each is a different way of looking at the question: Is vocational education the right choice for my child?

1. IS YOUR CHILD BEING "TRACKED" OR "SIDE-TRACKED" INTO VOCATIONAL EDUCATION? A disproportionate number of students "tracked" into vocational courses are minority students, "slow" learners, and students classified as having "behavior problems." The earlier this tracking occurs, the less likely it is that a student will reenter the academic curriculum. Ironically, an early start in a career may actually narrow the opportunities and limit the expectations of many vocational students.

   If your child wants a vocational program, he may benefit by enrolling in a vocational high school. Students in such specialized schools are better prepared than are students taking vocational course work within a comprehensive high school because vocational high schools tend to have a more experienced staff, closer links with the business community, in-depth programming, and superior equipment.

2. WHAT TYPE OF EQUIPMENT AND TECHNIQUES ARE BEING USED? Much of the equipment and techniques currently used in vocational programs are outdated. Often students trained in

school must be retrained in the "real" world. To solve this problem, money is needed for better equipment and teacher training. Some schools actively solicit corporations to make up the funding deficit. They point out that it is to the company's advantage to train students now, not later on "company time."

3. ARE EDUCATIONAL BASICS PART OF THE VOCATIONAL CURRICULUM? A vocational curriculum does not always stress reading, math, and writing. Yet these basics are important because they enable students to learn new skills and cope with an ever-changing job market. Today, big business annually spends almost $40 billion to educate workers who did not learn basic skills in secondary schools. Knowing *how* to learn is a lifetime necessity. It is your child's insurance policy for the future. Curriculum changes, but learning skills do not.

Today's kindergartners must be prepared to have six to ten careers (not jobs) in a lifetime! They will work a shorter work week: twenty hours rather than forty hours. Longer lifespans also mean your children will have more career decisions to make than you had. They may be returning to school once every six or seven years for occupation-related retraining. Students need the "basics" to help them cope with these changes as their skills become outdated.

4. IS YOUR CHILD IMPLICITLY TAUGHT THAT HIGH SCHOOL IS HIS LAST SCHOOL EXPERIENCE? Too often, vocational programs imply that further education is not essential. After all, the vocational student is not college bound. Yet salary increase and promotion often depend upon expertise in technology and mastery of a given field, which are achieved through ongoing education.

5. WHEN YOUR CHILD GRADUATES, WHERE AND HOW WILL HE BE EMPLOYED? WHAT SHOULD BE HIS REALISTIC EXPECTATIONS? *"Asked whether they preferred applicants with vocational or academic backgrounds, almost half of the employers (49 percent) said that they had no preference, about one-third (34 percent) preferred applicants who*

had been enrolled in academic curricula, and only 17 percent favored those with background in vocational education."

Vocational training does not increase job prospects. Students tend not to be employed in their field of training because of poor follow-up procedures, an unrealistic approach to the job market, and inadequate training on antiquated equipment. Those who find employment frequently become locked into no-growth, lower-paying jobs where earnings are limited. Initially, female graduates of business/office programs fare better, since many find higher-paying employment as secretaries. This initial edge decreases in time because of lack of upward mobility in most of these positions.

Businesses today want not only skilled workers, but also diplomas. A diploma indicates character traits to an employer. It shows that a student was able to complete a course of study, attend classes regularly, be punctual, and have a "good" record. Employers in a competitive job market often seek people who have more credentials, such as a college diploma, than really necessary. A vocational program may not be enough to give your child the competing edge.

6. ARE FOLLOW-UP SUPPORT SERVICES AVAILABLE TO YOUR CHILD AFTER GRADUATION? WHAT ARE THESE SERVICES? Graduating vocational students often do not have the career guidance and counseling given the college bound. Ironically, they are the group most in need of postgraduate support services. Determine what community programs exist for graduates of vocational training schools. These can include programs to develop job-finding skills, career-changing strategies, and educational options for advancement.

7. IS THE VOCATIONAL PROGRAM TRAINING ONLY BLUE-COLLAR WORKERS? Vocational education should stress upward mobility. Too often, course work focuses on making the student a skilled worker in only one area. Students should be taught management basics, such as accounting and finance, so that they can later make informed decisions if they choose to open

their own businesses (a beautician opening her own beauty shop, for example) or advance in their careers (a welder becomes union foreman).

8. IS YOUR CHILD RECEIVING PROPER GUID- ANCE? Academically as well as vocationally tracked students should be given accurate and "real-world" in- formation regarding career choices. Today there are over 90,000 job titles from which to choose. Students should receive appropriate guidance early and often in selecting course work. In this way they can keep their options open, stay attuned to "real-world" require- ments, and have a better chance of succeeding in a career field.

Even with a good education . . . the future job market for today's infants could be tight. With fewer people com- peting for jobs by the year 2007, entry level positions should be plentiful. But a trend toward later retirement will mean fewer advancement opportunities.

Where will the jobs be? *"The most widely accepted labor market projections call for the fastest growth in ser- vices, finance and trade; the greatest numbers of new jobs are expected in the areas of health services, computers, repair of business and industrial machines, banking, sec- retarial services and recreation.* [Other areas include medical science, energy production, food processing, construction, and building.] *Employees in most of these growth areas will need strong general skills, not job-spe- cific skills that can usually be learned in short-term, on- the-job training. Moreover, such job-specific skills, when taught in the classroom, are best taught in the post-sec- ondary programs or in separate vocational schools, not in comprehensive high schools.* The highest paying jobs will go to those who have skills that cannot be com- puterized or automated. These include athletes, artists, and writers. Second-tier salaries will be made by high technology workers.

There will be growth in jobs not specifically requir- ing college degrees. These positions include techni- cians in robotics, lasers, computers, housing rehabilitation, hazardous waste disposal, holography, and medicine; telemarketing sales people; and social workers involved in geriatrics. As much as 88 percent of the population may be involved in these service-related jobs—half in the information field.

The workplace will also be changing. People will be able to work from their homes because of interactive cable linked to central computers. A shorter work week will increase time for recreation and further education. There will be more job-sharing. Mobility will come from changing jobs, having more than one job, working as a consultant on limited projects, and entrepreneurial endeavors.

You and other adults are important role models. Share your work successes with your child. Discuss how you deal with difficult work situations and choices, as well as how you have dealt with failures. Most of all, share your dreams with your child and remember to let your child have his own dream—don't expect him to live yours.

9. WHAT ABOUT THE IMPORTANCE OF THE WORK ETHIC AND THE NECESSITY OF AFTER-SCHOOL EMPLOYMENT? According to *Life* magazine, more than a third of high school students aged 15–19 have some type of part time job where they work 15–20 hours per week. Both schools and parents should teach the importance of our society's work ethic. Employment, however, should not interfere with your child's academic learning. In the long run, academics studies will make him more successful than his after-school, minimum-wage job.

10. WHAT IS YOUR CHILD'S DREAM? Early tracking into vocational programs may deny your child his "dream." Student dreams are often unrealistic but can be an important motivator for learning, self-esteem, and self-expectations. All students should be allowed to dream.

To help your child realize his dream, help him develop a plan. Your child needs to learn what it takes to make the dream come true and what to do if it does not. Falling short of one's dreams is not failing. Failing to have dreams is the deepest failure of all.

HALLMARKS OF AN IDEAL
VOCATIONAL EDUCATIONAL PROGRAM

Use this checklist to rate your school's vocational program. If you are unsure of what the program offers, find out before your child enrolls in vocational education. If you desire more information, check with your school's guidance counselor or principal.

—— 1. Expert teachers
—— 2. Modern equipment
—— 3. Emphasis on the basics for learning: reading and computation, as well as skill development in specific vocational areas
—— 4. Follow-up and support services
—— 5. Guidance to explore different occupations
—— 6. Opportunity for future growth and job development
—— 7. Development of skills based on interests and aptitude
—— 8. Development of attitudes and habits that foster the work ethic
—— 9. Awareness of the necessity of post-secondary training and education

AMBITION, THE WORK ETHIC, AND RESPONSIBILITY

Ambition and the Child Who Is Not Immediately Attending College. Ambition does not have to culminate in going to college. If a child does not attend college or postpones it, he is not doomed to a life of poor earnings and poor future prospects. About 80 percent of all jobs in today's economy do not require a college degree. Whether your child decides to attend college or not, help him focus on a future direction for his life by discussing these points:

HELPING YOUR CHILD FOCUS ON THE FUTURE

1. Explore and encourage your child's interests. Help him recognize which of his interests would be useful in particular occupations.
2. What occupations interest your child?
3. Are your child's goals realistic for him to achieve?
4. Discuss your child's immediate future. What would he like to do when he graduates from high school?
5. Help your child plan the steps for achievement. Discuss what training is necessary to achieve his goals, what

earnings he can expect over time, and what extra education he may need in the future.

6. If your child is unwilling to focus upon any career path, find out why. Is he afraid of failure or of success? Discuss how he can overcome any weaknesses and rely on strengths to succeed.

7. Help build your child's confidence in his future. Encourage activities that bolster his self-image and add to his achievements.

8. Introduce your child to others currently working in areas of his interest. Let him "shadow" these people so he can learn firsthand what a job is like.

9. Discuss the realities and importance of being financially independent. How much is needed to live in a particular fashion? What can he expect from you regarding financial support? For how long?

10. Assure your child that career decisions are not engraved in stone. One person's career path may include many different and successful jobs and careers over a lifetime.

Ambition and College. If you definitely want your child to attend college, start preparing him well before his senior year in high school. If you wait until then, it may be too late.

PARENT ACTION *Preparing Your Child for College •* The following statements describe everyday situations in which you can help prepare your child for college. Rate yourself on each item by circling the number that best describes your support. If you score below a 3 on any item, make some changes in that area.

5	4	3	2	1
ALWAYS	VERY OFTEN	SOMETIMES	RARELY	NEVER

1. I share with my child the expectation that he can and should attend college. 5 4 3 2 1

2. I help my child see the relationship between college and his future goals and expectations. 5 4 3 2 1

3. I help my child choose the right high school course work for college preparation.   5   4   3   2   1

4. I monitor my child's classwork to make sure it is successfully completed.   5   4   3   2   1

5. I encourage my child to use good study habits.   5   4   3   2   1

6. I encourage my child to participate in extracurricular activities, as well as to achieve good academic marks.   5   4   3   2   1

7. I have made sure that my child has received proper guidance in selecting a college where he will be most successful.   5   4   3   2   1

8. If necessary, I have arranged extra help for my child to prepare him for national college entrance tests.   5   4   3   2   1

9. My child and I have made financial arrangements so that he can attend college.   5   4   3   2   1

10. My child and I have explored financial assistance and scholarships that he may be qualified to receive from local groups and colleges.   5   4   3   2   1

THREE

AFTER-SCHOOL TIME: HOMEWORK, STUDYING, AND TELEVISION

After-school activities vary from child to child. Some children may participate in extracurricular activities such as athletics, debating, hobby and service clubs, music and art programs. These and similar activities encourage responsibility, teach valuable skills, improve self-esteem, and may lead to lifetime careers and hobbies. No matter what children do, they all get homework, they all must study, and they all watch some television. It is important for you to help your child achieve the proper balance between homework, study, and television.

HOMEWORK AND STUDYING

Many times children, and even parents, question why teachers assign homework. It is given for several reasons: to reinforce skills learned, to improve skills, to increase knowledge, and to connect the school world with the home. Homework can involve listening skills, note-taking, memory development, report writing, or group projects. The best homework is that which is individualized for a student's own needs, reviewed in class, and returned promptly with appropriate corrections and comments. These comments should include praise and encouragement.

Forty percent of the public believes that not enough homework is assigned to elementary school students. According to 47 percent of the public, not enough homework is given to secondary school students. The public may be right. The amount of homework today is 50 percent less than it was in the early 1960s. Two-thirds of high school seniors report that the work assigned takes one hour per night. Even this amount of homework is often not completed. Assigning more homework will not benefit a child unless he does the homework. Parents should monitor homework, not do it. If a child does not have a formal homework assignment, he may have studying to complete.

PARENT ACTION *How You Can Help Your Child with Homework* • The following statements describe everyday situations in which you can improve your child's homework habits. Rate yourself on each item by circling the number that best reflects your support. If you score below a 3 on any item, make some changes in that area.

5	4	3	2	1
ALWAYS	VERY OFTEN	SOMETIMES	RARELY	NEVER

1. I have provided a well-lit, comfortable study area for my child to use for homework and studying.   5 4 3 2 1

2. I limit household noise, sibling interference, TV watching, and other distractions that interfere with homework and studying.   5 4 3 2 1

3. I ask my child if he has any homework to complete.   5 4 3 2 1

4. I allow time within the family schedule for completion of assignments.   5 4 3 2 1

5. I encourage my child to do homework daily, at a specific time of day.   5 4 3 2 1

6. I review assignments, classwork brought home, and the school day with my child.   5 4 3 2 1

Your child should be able to relate the homework assignment to classwork already covered or to be covered shortly.

7. I help my child organize assignments by encouraging him to use a book or envelope for all assignments. *Here he can note due dates of all homework, how it is to be submitted, and what is required.* 5 4 3 2 1

8. I help my child anticipate how long an assignment or studying should take to avoid last-minute rush jobs and all-nighters. 5 4 3 2 1

9. I encourage my child to ask questions when assignments are given to make sure he understands what is expected. 5 4 3 2 1

10. If my child cannot explain or understand the homework, I find out why. *For example, was he inattentive in class? Was the assignment given at the dismissal bell?* 5 4 3 2 1

11. I initiate and maintain contact with my child's teacher(s), to learn about his progress. 5 4 3 2 1

12. I solicit help from my child's teachers. *This can include learning about skill-building techniques, follow-through methods, educational activities, and games.* 5 4 3 2 1

13. I encourage my child to discuss what he is learning from an assignment. *This stresses its importance and value.* 5 4 3 2 1

14. I help my child with drills and practice and, if appropriate or possible, do sample problems analogous to the ones assigned. 5 4 3 2 1

15. If my child says he can't do an assignment, I discuss the work with him. *Verbalization increases retention, encourages understanding, and promotes recall. If appropriate, I help my child list rules, information given, information wanted, and the order of steps needed to complete the assignment.* 5 4 3 2 1

16. I encourage my child to check homework. *Sloppy work results in wrong answers and increases the time needed for completion.* 5 4 3 2 1

17. If my child asks me to, I check homework   5   4   3   2   1
for neatness and completeness. I do not
correct my child's homework. *A child
learns best by making his own corrections.*

18. If I recognize errors in an assignment, I   5   4   3   2   1
ask my child to review the work.

19. I impress upon my child that first efforts   5   4   3   2   1
may not produce the best work he is capa-
ble of achieving and that he should try
again.

20. If my child is reluctant to do homework, I   5   4   3   2   1
motivate him by praise, and granting privi-
leges.

21. I have high expectations for my child and   5   4   3   2   1
share them with him.

22. I give my child a sense of pride in his   5   4   3   2   1
schoolwork and in himself through praise
and compliments.

23. I encourage my child to complete assign-   5   4   3   2   1
ments on one subject at a time. *This pro-
motes efficient use of time, concentration,
and a sense of accomplishment.*

24. I sign my child's homework assignments   5   4   3   2   1
and tests when requested by the teacher.

25. I know the procedure for absent students   5   4   3   2   1
to make up assignments or tests and to get
notes.

STUDY SKILLS

Study skills aid in the gathering of information and ideas
through reading and listening. Good study skills enable a student
to record information through notetaking, outlining, and sum-
marizing. The student is then able to make sense of the new information by synthesizing and organizing the information. Good
study skills will aid in memory retention and assist in the utiliza-
tion of new information and ideas.

• • •

PARENT ACTION *How You Can Help Your Child with Studying Strategies* • The following statements describe everyday situations in which you can improve your child's study habits. Rate yourself on each item by circling the number that best reflects your support. If you score below a 3 on any item, make some changes in that area.

5	4	3	2	1
ALWAYS	VERY OFTEN	SOMETIMES	RARELY	NEVER

1. I encourage my child to use these methods: **5 4 3 2 1**
   - **Review study sheets.**
   - **Recall appropriate methods and rules for problem solving.**
   - **Summarize and recite facts.**
   - **Use mnemonic devices to help remember facts.**
   - **Take notes.**
   - **Underline and identify key words.**
   - **Outline main ideas.**
   - **Self-test.**

2. I encourage my child to study for several days **5 4 3 2 1**
   instead of one long night the day before the test.

3. I discuss testing procedures with my child. I **5 4 3 2 1**
   ask the following questions:
   - **What material will be covered?**
   - **What types of questions are going to be asked?**
   - **What type of test is it (objective or essay)?**
   - **How does this particular test relate to your grade?**
   - **Will there be a class review prior to the test?**
   - **Has the teacher suggested how to study for the test?**
   - **What are the make-up policies if you are absent on test day?**

• • •

4. I encourage my child to practice relaxation techniques.   5   4   3   2   1

5. I boost my child's confidence by helping him build and realize high expectations. I support my child's efforts and expectations to succeed.   5   4   3   2   1

6. If my child asks me, I help him review for a test.   5   4   3   2   1

7. I encourage improvement in my child. I remind him that past failures are not predictors of future failures.   5   4   3   2   1

TELEVISION AND SCHOOL

"The teachings of television are hostile to language and language development, hostile to vigorous intellectual activity, hostile to both science and history, hostile to social order, and hostile in a general way to conceptualization. Television is a curriculum that stresses inconstancy, not constancy; discontinuity, not coherence; immediate, not deferred gratification; emotional, not intellectual response."

How does watching television affect our children? Experts say this about television viewing:

- One-dimensional portrayal of relationships on television desensitizes children to understanding "real" relationships and emotions.
- A Michigan State University study found that one-third of four- and five-year-olds, given a hypothetical choice between giving up television or their fathers, chose to keep the TV.
- TV watching is a passive activity. There is no interaction; therefore, little can be learned through "real" experience.
- No creativity is involved. All is "given"; nothing is left to the imagination. To satisfy the viewer, almost all episodic serials are neatly and faultlessly concluded within a tidy hour. Today, TV is in color, but it usually presents answers in black and white.
- For dramatic reasons, television portrays extremes in behavior. People rarely are shown thinking before acting.
- TV is designed for everyone. Vocabulary is often simple. Characterization is often stagnant and stereotyped.

- TV encourages unhealthy consumerism.
- TV disturbs brain patterns. After prolonged television watching a viewer's brain goes into the alpha state of deep relaxation. This explains why, when called away from the TV, a child may be irritable as though arising from sleep. It also explains why so many of us fall asleep with the set on!

How much time do most children spend watching television?

Elementary School TV Statistics
- The average two- to five-year-old spends 28 hours a week watching TV.
- Kindergarten graduates have already seen 5,000 TV hours. That is more time than is required to complete a B.A. degree.
- Grade school students watch 30 hours of TV a week.
- Students watching no more than 2 hours of television a day read above average for their age groups. Six or more hours of television viewing per day correlate with lower reading proficiency.
- The average cartoon includes 26 incidents of violence.
- The lexicon of most television programs is less than 5,000 words. This is about the same size vocabulary of a child just entering school.

Junior High TV Statistics
- By age 12, a child has seen 100,000 violent TV episodes; 13,000 people destroyed.
- Lower achievers tend to watch more TV. This is self-defeating because they need more time to study and learn.
- Aggressive children "act up" more when viewing TV shows portraying violent acts.

High School TV Statistics
- By the time a student graduates from high school, he has watched 15,000 TV hours as compared to the 11,000 hours he has spent in school.
- By age 18, a child has watched 22,000 hours of TV.
- By the age of 20, an American child will have seen 700,000 TV commercials, at a rate of about 700 per week.

How would your child view the world if television were his only source of input? To get an idea, consider the validity of these statements about the "real world" as seen through the eye of the television camera.

The World According to Television

- Television depicts and communicates superficial knowledge.
- Television shows give a distorted picture of occupations and work.
- Television shows often communicate that successful human relationships require manipulation of others.
- Detailed scenes portraying how crimes are committed are commonplace. It is believed that some juvenile crime may be inspired by TV.
- Violence is an everyday experience. Many TV shows indicate that because the law cannot deal with crime, independent citizen action is necessary.
- The TV world is often rotten and dangerous.
- Racial and sexist put-downs are portrayed as witty on television.
- Television shows portray adults as dummies; children know best.
- Women, as portrayed on television, are inferior to men.
- Television communicates the message that life and education should always be entertaining.
- Drinking is great. It enhances performance.
- Material things will make people happy and gratification should be instantaneous.
- Schools are a waste of time and have nothing to offer.
- Man-woman relationships are always sexual.
- Taking the right over-the-counter drug makes you feel better and happier.
- Eating sugared snacks or cereal is good.
- Women should always dress to please men. Women please their families by cleaning and cooking for them.
- Athletics is a serious business. Anyone can become a star.
- Musical ability is all that is needed for success. It is easy for talent to be discovered.
- Men know how to fix cars, paint, and manage finances. They should handle these things.

- Older people should be considered only insofar as they affect the young.
- People should drive cars very fast and recklessly.
- Stunts are easy. They can be tried without getting hurt.
- Death occurs very violently and affects hardly anyone but the person who is killed.

The Value of Television Should you throw out your television set or never turn it on again? Wait. There *are* advantages to watching TV. Recent studies indicate that:

- Watching television from one to ten hours a week has a positive effect. The reason for this is unclear. It could be that those who limit their watching discriminate more by selecting higher-quality shows. They may also be using their non-television time for more academic purposes.
- Educational TV can be beneficial and is further enhanced by interaction. When selecting TV shows in which to invest time, choose those that have the most to offer in the areas of science, adventure, biography, music, or drama; or just pick a well-written, well-acted show for humor and sheer enjoyment. Laughter and relaxation are important for everyone's mental health.

PARENT ACTION *How You Can Help Your Child Develop Healthy Television Habits* • It would be impractical to suggest to parents of school-aged children to forbid all television watching. But here's what you can do to limit the time your child spends in front of the TV, and improve the quality of the time he does watch.

- SET AN EXAMPLE. Children of parents who do not watch TV excessively tend to watch less TV themselves.
- LIMIT ALL TV WATCHING by the whole family. Make a commitment together. Form a plan to limit TV watching for a week. Discuss reactions, results, and alternatives after the time is up. How was your time spent? What programs did you really miss? Why?
- LOG TV WATCHING HABITS. Becoming aware of your habits will make everyone more critical and sensitive to choices and use of time.

55

- MODIFY TV WATCHING in small ways, if you and your family cannot go "cold turkey." Begin with some of these rules:
  - TV may be watched for only an hour on school nights.
  - TV is limited for each person to a certain number of hours per week.
  - TV may not be watched at mealtimes.
  - Only TV specials of educational value may be watched. Try to get your child to talk with you about what constitutes "educational value." You may get into some amusing discussions!
  - TV may be watched if someone is sick.
  - TV may be watched at a friend's home.
  - All TV watching must be scheduled in advance and posted on a "public" calendar with date, day, hour, channel, initials, and reason for watching. This will make you and your children plan viewing and time commitments more carefully.
- MONITOR YOUR CHILD'S VIEWING. Watch any program that may be controversial or scary with your child. One study found that when children view TV with an experienced person who comments on events, defines vocabulary, and reflects on the values shown, children apply these elements to their own lives in a more positive way.
- DISCUSS TELEVISION PROGRAMS that you watch.
  - Reserve time to critique programs: "Were they worthwhile?"
  - Link TV programs to the "real world": "Were they accurate in portraying people?"
  - Link TV programs to academic endeavors: "How can we find out more about that? Was the portrayal of that person historically accurate?"
  - Link TV programs to real emotions and feelings: "Would you do the same thing in that situation? Why? Why not?"
  - Critique commercials: "To whom does this product appeal? Why?"
- DO NOT CONSTANTLY USE THE TV as an electronic babysitter. If you're generally careful about TV viewing, however, you don't have to feel guilty about using the TV for this purpose once in a while. Just remember that find-

ing answers to problems such as whining or boredom is ultimately a parent's job. Television is not the best solution.

- DO NOT BECOME INTIMIDATED by your children's wishes to watch television. Let them know why you're limiting television time and stress that it's not a punishment. Setting an example for your children is important.
- DO NOT EXPECT COMPLIANCE with a "TV Limit" rule if you do not help your child in pursuing other interests. New pastimes do not have to be as "entertaining" as TV, but they should involve your child in productive, imaginative projects. Before "laying down the law," think how to channel and challenge your child (and yourself) with this newfound time. Be prepared to give of your time and interest. Your activities may include:
  - Leisure pursuits: Reading, socializing, cultivating hobbies, or listening to music.
  - Creative pursuits: Involve your child as a participant. Family projects may include making music, art, dance; keeping an album or journal.
  - Communication: Use this time to talk with your child. Rediscover the lost but worthwhile art of conversation!
  - Academic pursuits: Reading, studying, developing skills, building vocabulary. When learning new skills, younger children (ages two to seven) especially benefit from working one-on-one with an adult.
- DO NOT LEAVE THE TV ON as constant background.

SPECIAL PROGRAMS

Besides the basic academic and elective courses, schools also offer a variety of special programs to meet the needs of select student populations. These programs may have been mandated or may have evolved from local community needs. Special programs may include classes for the learning disabled, special education for the mentally or physically handicapped, and classes for gifted or bilingual students.

Special programs often engender heated controversy. Proponents of special programs want not only equal opportunity for students enrolled in these classes but also equal results. Equal opportunity requires providing additional learning time, teacher-training, and resources. Those in favor of special programs believe it is better for society to pay now in school for this special instruction than to pay more later for illiteracy, prisons, and welfare.

Although education cannot guarantee equal results, it can and should provide equal opportunities to learn. Each child has the right to succeed according to his abilities. Good education allows each student his best chance to develop skills. By educating all the children to the best of their abilities, schools provide the greatest benefit to all segments of society. To better understand the benefits and purposes of special programs, we need to examine them individually.

ABILITY GROUPING:
A PROGRAM TO HELP ALL LEARNERS

Ability grouping, or tracking, is group placement of students according to their abilities in particular subjects. (This is not to be confused with programs that place students in a long-term, separate curriculum program based on such broad labels as "vocational" or "college-bound.") On the elementary school level, for example, reading groups are a form of ability grouping. In secondary schools, such grouping may be determined by the class subject, such as Algebra 1: Section C, Algebra 1: Section D, in which students learn the same material but at a different pace. The practice of grouping sparks controversy, often polarizing teachers and parents.

ABILITY GROUPING: GOOD OR BAD?

PRO	CON
Cultivates the best and brightest	Creates an educational elite
Creates future leaders	Makes "bosses" and "workers"
Cannot track all students the same way because they have different abilities	Education can make up differences in ability, if all students are given equal opportunity and access to learn
Too costly to society if ability groupings are not done in school	Too costly to the schools now
Can help gifted, quicker learners; less frustration for slow learners	Lowers the quality of education for those not in the same classes as those with greater ability
Allows for more efficient use of time and resources	Time and resources are unfairly allocated; "poorer" students receive poorer, less motivated teachers and instruction
Creates and maintains high standards	Overall, lowers curriculum and standards
Gives "poorer" students work they can do, so fewer drop out	Lower-tracked students know their placement, so they are more likely to drop out

Allows special groups to benefit from specially designed programs	Lower tracks tend to be filled with minority students, lower economic groups
Raises expectation levels and self-esteem, since students are taught on a level at which they can be successful	Groupings lower expectations, self-esteem, incentive, and motivation
Makes students easier to teach, manage classwork for, promote	Does not consider individual instruction needs, mastery learning

Whatever the validity of the pros and cons, grouping and tracking occur extensively both in and out of the classroom:

- Students themselves track one another. They know who is considered bright and who is not. Students can be ruthless. They expect some of their peers to excel or fail in certain areas, and they label them accordingly as the basketball star, the math whiz, the know-it-all, the dummy, or the class goof-off.
- Many of the special programs that benefit minority or special students the most can be considered a type of tracking. Ironically, these are often the very programs that critics of tracking insist upon for the "educationally disadvantaged." (It can be argued that even the term "educationally disadvantaged" labels and "tracks" a group of students.)
- Teachers, students, and parents all talk about tracking. This often occurs subconsciously:
  "Jane is good in math."
  "Jack excels in basketball."
  "Nancy cannot draw a straight line."
- Tracking may occur even in a situation that is thought to be "tracking-free." Some students' abilities lead teachers to expect more of them in different areas, such as oral presentation, or written research reports. These students may be treated differently from their peers when given the same tasks.

If your child is involved in an ability-grouped course, consider and understand the purposes of that program. Ideally, tracking is

60

monitored, encourages mobility, and allows for frequent evaluations of student progress. In this way, students are not stuck in a track until it becomes a rut, precluding opportunities for their development, progress, and success.

SPECIAL EDUCATION

Special education is for children with physical or intellectual handicaps including those diagnosed as mentally retarded or emotionally disturbed. Almost 12 percent of the school population is in a special education program. These programs may include children with several combinations of learning disorders. Their learning problems may be psychological, perceptual, or the results of brain injury, minimal brain dysfunction, or dyslexia/developmental aphasia. Meeting the special education needs of such children is ensured by the Handicapped Children's Act, which has three major points:

1. All handicapped children have the right to the same free public education available to all other American children.
2. Parents are entitled to challenge a school's treatment of handicapped children.
3. Schools must make every effort to merge handicapped children into the regular school program.

Critics of mainstreaming programs question the practice of removing handicapped children from therapeutic settings to become marginal members of regular classrooms. Proponents reply that these handicapped children, too, are entitled to an equal education.

It has been estimated that physically, emotionally, and intellectually handicapped students represent about 10 to 13 percent of the student population. The government has allocated greater funding to special populations. The average cost to educate a handicapped student is three to four times greater than educating a regular student. Those with greater handicaps can cost even more.

School provides guidance, diagnosis, and an Individualized Educational Program (IEP) to enable handicapped children to develop and maximize their abilities. You, in turn, must provide proper and consistent support at home.

61

LEARNING DISABILITIES

Learning disabilities is a broad term used to describe a diverse group of children who exhibit problems in the basic psychological processes involved in understanding or in using spoken or written language. These may be manifested in disorders of listening, thinking, talking, reading, writing, spelling, or arithmetic. They do not include learning problems which are due primarily to visual, hearing, or motor handicaps, to mental retardation, emotional disturbances, or environmental disadvantages.

It is estimated that there are more than 12 percent of all school children classified as learning disabled. A child may be suspected of being learning disabled if he demonstrates a significant discrepancy between achievement, usually in reading, and ability compared with a child of the same age, intelligence, and experience. If you suspect your child has a learning disability, advise the school and request a psycho-educational evaluation. Tests are administered by a school psychologist to diagnose and measure some of the problems. These same tests are also used to rule out other causes that can contribute to a learning problem. Lastly, both teacher and parent can observe the child in a variety of learning situations to understand if there is a pattern in his schooling difficulties.

It is important for a parent of a learning disabled child to understand his child's limitations and problems. These include:

- A child with learning disabilities does not "grow out" of his learning problems. Be prepared to see he gets the help he needs at school and at home.
- A learning disabled child, if not identified early, is often a failure in school. Screening for a learning disability can be done as early as kindergarten or the first grade in elementary school.
- A learning disabled child must be taught in an appropriate manner. Trained teachers of the learning disabled will work with your child. He must learn to cope with, adjust to, and compensate for his disabilities.
- If your child is diagnosed as having a learning disability, it is imperative for you to be involved in his education and assiduously to monitor his progress. Keep the school informed of progress and setbacks at home.

• Federal and state law guarantees your child the right to a free and appropriate public school education. It is up to you to assure that your learning disabled child receives the maximum benefit of these laws through the programs available in your school district.

THE GIFTED CHILD

How do you know if your child is gifted? A child who is talented is exceptionally able in one area. A child who is gifted is exceptionally able in many areas. In general, 3 to 5 percent of all the student population is classified as gifted. Whether gifted or not, the student should be supported by parents and teachers for his own particular abilities.

Once, IQ (Intelligence Quotient) tests were the main criteria for determining who was gifted. An IQ score measured the difference in intelligence between a child's chronological age and mental age. IQ scores are no longer the only determinant of giftedness. Research indicates that IQ tests do not reveal all the specific areas, such as leadership or organizational skills, where students are gifted. Furthermore, IQ tests may be culturally biased. Today's gifted students are identified by observation and expert judgment, as well as by IQ scores. But the task of identification is formidable for both parents and educators.

What traits of "giftedness" do you see in your child? On the next page, check the ones that your child possesses. As you read each trait, recall examples of when and how your child showed this ability. Do not be surprised to learn that your child is more gifted than you thought. On the other hand, do not be overly hasty to label your child as a genius in all things!

Recognizing Your Child's Gifts
1. Has above-average abilities in several areas.

*EXAMPLE*_____

_____

2. Shows commitment to tasks by being goal oriented.

*EXAMPLE*_____

_____

3. Demonstrates creativity.

*EXAMPLE*_____

_____

4. Shows a drive to achieve by being persistent.

*EXAMPLE*_____

_____

5. Exhibits self-confidence.

*EXAMPLE*_____

_____

6. Uses abstract thinking and is eager to understand relationships.

*EXAMPLE*_____

_____

7. Has a good memory.

*EXAMPLE*_____

_____

8. Is exceptionally curious.

*EXAMPLE*_____

_____

9. Possesses and uses an extensive vocabulary.

*EXAMPLE*_____

_____

10. Tackles several tasks or projects at the same time.

*EXAMPLE*_____

_____

Even if your child is gifted and is performing well in his school-work, he still may exhibit negative behaviors. These can occur for reasons that often seem contradictory. For example:

- Your child withdraws from friends and family because he feels misunderstood.
- He is easily frustrated, lazy, restless, or bored because his work is "too easy."
- He is so intent upon resolving a particular problem that he will react rudely to interruptions. Alternate activities, even "fun" ones, are often met with disfavor. He may also be resistant to routines that conflict with his own personal projects and timetables. They seem unimportant to him.
- Your child may dominate conversations with friends and adults. He may be highly critical of others because of his belief that he is more knowledgeable.

It is important for schools to educate the gifted. A gifted student can master the standard curriculum in one-third the usual time. Time spent on a subject in class is allotted in the following way: 70 percent for mastering the basics; 30 percent for higher cognitive processes. The gifted child requires the reverse formulation. Yet, there are some who do not believe in additional funding for programs for gifted children. They maintain that these students already have an advantage and do not need more, but if schools do not fund gifted programs, the result is often "bright flight." Gifted students flee public schools for private ones that offer the enriched courses they desire. This lowers public schools' overall quality. The following strategies have been employed by schools to meet the needs of gifted children:

- Acceleration to the next grade.
- Telescoping two grades into one year.
- Curriculum enrichment.
- Independent study.
- Credit by examination.
- Tracking or ability grouping.
- Special programs for gifted students.

Being labeled gifted is not enough for a child to develop all his potential. According to *A Nation at Risk:* "Over half the population of gifted students do not match their tested ability with comparable achievement in school." Development of a child's talents requires long-term commitment. Family support is the most integral part of this process. According to Benjamin S. Bloom in his book *Developing Talent in Young People,* there are some common traits of families that produce successful, gifted children. These strategies used by the parents of gifted children can be used successfully by all parents to ensure their child's success in school.

1. These families are hardworking and active. Work takes precedence over play. Even play often involves purposeful activities, such as practice and learning. Wasting time or shirking responsibilities is viewed with strong disapproval. Parents are positive role models.

2. In most cases, parents actively share in their child's activities and interests. As spectators, these parents critique and appreciate their child's performance in terms of how the child's skill or knowledge improved.

3. Parents firmly believe in doing one's best. They are openly proud of their own achievements. Trying hard and doing well are discussed with children and are expected. Parents set high standards.

4. Children are supervised and corrected in activities. Parents involve children in their activities, such as vacation planning, running household errands, attending concerts, going to exhibits and museums, and hobbies.

5. Family time is organized and scheduled so that other demands do not interfere with the practice of concentration required for development of talent.

6. Parents willingly and joyfully participate in their child's area of interest. When parents and children share the same interests, a closer relationship can develop. The field of interests often dominates conversation, as well as family activities.

7. Parents value and respect their child's talent. They help him focus his efforts on this talent. They are quick to give approval and attention. They encourage their child to think about future success. Often a child is encouraged to show written work or perform for others. Thus, a child believes that he is unique and that the activity he is pursuing is worthwhile. Evidence of the child's accom-

plishments, such as records or trophies, are kept and displayed. Parents also provide resources and materials. This requires a commitment of both time and money. Parents attend all meets, recitals, or competitions in which their child participates. These events enable a child to compete and measure his skills against those of his peers. Such participation also rewards his work and gives him further incentive and motivation to pursue his goals.

8. Initially, instruction is provided by a teacher or coach who is enthusiastic and works well with children. Later, instruction is provided by a more accomplished professional. The parents work together with the teacher to reinforce learned skills. Parents learn what the teacher's standards are and supervise their child's practice, preparation time, and effort, so that he can do his best. This teaches the child discipline.

9. If progress falters, solutions and discussions are immediately sought. Encouragement is always offered. Failure is discussed in terms of how one can improve performance for next time.

10. These parents describe their gifted child as persistent, competitive, and eager. This child may not be the most talented, but he is often the most motivated. He learns to set goals and pace himself because he is enthusiastic and willing to work to develop his talent.

How You Can Help Your Gifted Child Though these strategies are useful in dealing with gifted children, they are also valid for *all* children.

1. Do not pressure; do not overschedule or exploit your child's gifts.
2. Encourage your child to take risks. The gifted are accustomed to excelling and being the best. They may be reluctant to try something new or unfamiliar, especially if the results initially seem uncertain or mediocre.
3. Provide enriching experiences, activities, opportunities, materials and, when appropriate, private instruction. The gifted child is often blocked by restrictions on curiosity, interruptions, the elimination of fantasy play, con-

stant comparison, lack of feedback, use of prepared material, and the imposition of others' ideas.

4. Do not allow your child to neglect the physical in his pursuit of intellectual achievement. (Neither should you allow your child to neglect the intellectual in pursuit of physical achievements!)

5. Help your child cope with being gifted. The gifted may face rejection by their peers, resentment by teachers, awkward relationships with siblings, annoyance from adults. They often feel lonely, ridiculed, and undesirable. If these emotions predominate, a gifted child may become an underachiever in his desire to be like everyone else. Allow your gifted child to associate with intellectual peers instead of chronological peers.

6. Love your gifted child for himself, not for his abilities or accomplishments.

BILINGUAL EDUCATION

Bilingual education legislation arose out of the Civil Rights Act of 1964: "No person in the United States shall, on the ground of race, color, or national origin, be excluded from participation in, be denied the benefits of, or be subjected to discrimination under any program or activity receiving federal financial assistance."

Today there are more than sixty different language programs using bilingual techniques. In bilingual education programs, the student is taught reading and writing in his own language until English is mastered. Ideally, bilingual students learn the history, culture, and values of both languages. Classes try to maintain the "old culture," while encouraging students to develop skills in the new one.

Proponents of bilingual education believe " . . . in the earliest years of education, the mastery of language and skillful use of English is the most critically important goal we have to achieve." Many educators would agree with that statement, but they disagree on the best methods to achieve that goal. "We have unwisely embarked upon a policy of so-called 'bilingualism,' putting foreign language in competition with our own. English has long been the main uniting force of the American people. But now prolonged bilingual education in public schools . . . threatens to divide us along language lines."

To answer this charge, bilingual proponents must address the following problems:

- What should be the community's role in bilingual education?
- How should progress be measured?
- How can the bilingual curriculum be made richer and equivalent to the English-language curriculum?
- Will bilingual "graduates" be able to function, work, and succeed in the English-speaking world?
- How well should a child function in English to be mainstreamed into the English curriculum?
- What guidelines should be used for exit competencies from bilingual classes?

An alternative to bilingual education is the intensive, English-only method of "English as a Second Language." ESL relies on total immersion in English so that a student will learn rapidly and be able to particpate in the course work of other curriculum areas. This technique is most often used by government, universities, foreign medical schools, and private language schools.

Hispanics comprise the largest non-English-speaking population in school enrollment. In this decade there has also been a rapid increase in the number of Asian immigrants, representing many languages not often known, taught, or offered in teacher education courses. Yet federal law requires that children who speak any of seventy-four native languages are entitled to instruction in that language in public schools. Minority school enrollment is predicted to almost double to 30 percent in the next decade.

To meet the needs of these children, schools need to attract more qualified teachers who are skilled in a variety of languages. Yet even that will not meet the growing demand. Greater support is needed especially from parents, successful immigrants, and ethnic community leaders who are willing to share their knowledge and time to build a successful school-based program.

MOTIVATING YOUR CHILD
TO SUCCEED

W e in the United States believe in education. We have
high expectations for our schools and students. Yet many of us also
distrust our schools. These conflicting attitudes have a significant
impact on how teachers, parents, and students perceive themselves, how they act and feel, and what their expectations are. If
our school system is to be successful, it needs positive support and
high expectations from the community it serves.

It is up to parents to explain the purpose of school, the necessity
for education, and the importance of knowledge. Parents need to
help their child maintain focus, motivation, self-image, and a
sense of self-expectation. But ultimately, it is the child's own efforts that determine how well educated he becomes. You should
tell your children that education pays. American education is free.
Tell your child to get his money's worth—it is the best bargain
around. Education increases one's choices in life, maximizes opportunities, and gives skills upon which to build one's future.
Teachers need students who come to school with a positive attitude
that is continuously nurtured at home. From this base, teachers
can then give students the skills they need for success.

Children should not be burdened by their parents' past failures, unfulfilled hopes, or negative life-scripts. A parent's fears and doubts are contagious. A parent's indifference and apathy are also contagious. Give your child the will and motivation to learn. Set a positive tone. Children should aim to excel in school, not just to get by. High expectations are the foundation for learning, and they should be maintained in all areas of a child's life.

Students' enthusiasm for school diminishes with age. Why? There are many answers to this question. As your child grows older he becomes more prone to peer pressure and other societal distractions. Your child's focus on what is important may shift away from school-related areas toward peer mandates. The shift is away from what you as a parent emphasize toward peer-oriented activities. This is all the more reason you must work at keeping your child focused and motivated toward school. Parents' failure to maintain high expectations for their child results in failure for their child.

You remember your child's earliest achievements: when he learned to walk and to speak his first words. What was your reaction? You probably smiled, praised, and encouraged your child. That same expression of parental approval and pride is still important as your child grows and progresses through school. The following example illustrates what happens when expectations are lowered. The situation is not meant to be typical of all parents; however, it is far too common.

In the beginning of their child's school years, parents greet the child at the door with "How was school today? Is that your art project? What a wonderful idea!" Praise predominates.

In later grades, a child may be greeted at the door with, "You left your room a mess this morning. Don't throw your books on the table. Why did you wear that shirt to school?" Criticism predominates.

Which greeting would you prefer? Which would motivate you to do well in school? Not only does criticism detract from motivation, but it also has a negative impact on self-image, which affects the level of self-expectation. Positive criticism, concern, and support help a child maintain his self-image, achieve a proper sense of self-expectation, and remain motivated. Your child will have high expectations if he has a positive self-image.

Self-image involves self-confidence and self-worth. People behave in ways that are consistent with their self-images and with their own expectations and those of others. "What a person thinks of himself will determine his destiny."

PARENT ACTION *Building a Child's Self-Image* • Do you enhance your child's home environment to support learning? How often? The following statements identify everyday situations in which you can contribute to your child's learning. Rate yourself on each item by circling the number that best indicates how frequently you give your support. If you score below a 3 on any item, make some changes in that area.

5	4	3	2	1
ALWAYS	VERY OFTEN	SOMETIMES	RARELY	NEVER

1. I encourage my child to make decisions. 5 4 3 2 1
2. I recognize my child's contributions. 5 4 3 2 1
3. I do not judge my child according to invalid standards. I make allowances for my child's age and experience. 5 4 3 2 1
4. I help my child assume responsibilities to others and for himself. 5 4 3 2 1
5. I do not compare my child to others. 5 4 3 2 1
6. I encourage participation in activities that build a success pattern. 5 4 3 2 1
7. I help my child recognize, develop, and use his skills and talents. 5 4 3 2 1
8. I take pride in my child's accomplishments. I display work and brag! 5 4 3 2 1
9. I show appreciation by acknowledging my child's good qualities. 5 4 3 2 1
10. I share my personal image-building experiences with my child. 5 4 3 2 1
11. I read and tell stories to my child about well-known, successful people, family and friends. 5 4 3 2 1
12. I nurture a positive attitude in all tasks. 5 4 3 2 1
13. I encourage my child to vocalize his accomplishments to himself and others. 5 4 3 2 1
14. I encourage my child to keep records, trophies, journals, etc., of what he plans, thinks, and does. 5 4 3 2 1

15. I help my child build an internal positive   5 4 3 2 1
self-image by helping him change externally. I support safe weight loss/gain programs, aerobics, fitness programs, exercise, sports, proper nutrition, and relaxation techniques.

PARENT ACTION *Twenty Communication Tips for Image Building* • Do you enhance your child's home environment to support learning? How often? The following statements identify everyday situations in which you can contribute to your child's learning. Rate yourself on each item by circling the number that best indicates how frequently you give your support. If you score below a 3 on any item, make some changes in that area.

5	4	3	2	1
ALWAYS	VERY OFTEN	SOMETIMES	RARELY	NEVER

1. I extend to my children the common courtesies of listening that I use with everyone else. I do not interrupt; I do not use sarcasm, ridicule, put-downs, orders, ultimatums, or threats.   5 4 3 2 1

2. Whenever we talk, I acknowledge my feelings and my child's feelings.   5 4 3 2 1

3. I respond actively to my child by vocalizing and by using body language, gestures, and facial expressions.   5 4 3 2 1

4. I ask open-ended, not "yes/no" questions to encourage communication.   5 4 3 2 1

5. I solicit and value my child's opinions.   5 4 3 2 1

6. I ask questions about my child's hobbies, interests, and "passions."   5 4 3 2 1

7. I broaden my child's interests by helping him relate them to other areas; e.g., cars to physics, transportation, or the economy; clothing to design, marketing, or the history of fashion.   5 4 3 2 1

8. I include my children in conversations with adults and with other family members.   5 4 3 2 1

9. I discuss many topics with my child: family matters, controversial issues, emotional issues, current events, the future, the "whys." I do not give my child adult-sized problems, but I do not talk down to him either.   5 4 3 2 1

10. I plan both "quality" and "quantity" time to talk with my child.   5 4 3 2 1

11. I use bedtime conversation, dinner table discussion, etc., to talk with my child.   5 4 3 2 1

12. I optimize time for discussion during daily routines, such as car trips, shopping, etc.   5 4 3 2 1

13. If I am traveling, separated, or divorced, I "phone home" to talk to my child. I know problems cannot be solved at a distance, but a receptive ear is a good start.   5 4 3 2 1

14. I encourage my child to talk with other family members and friends.   5 4 3 2 1

15. I keep establishing rapport with my child by doing things together.   5 4 3 2 1

16. My child and I play games requiring communication skills.   5 4 3 2 1

17. I set a good communication example because I am aware of the influence of my own speech patterns and vocabulary.   5 4 3 2 1

18. I encourage my child to speak in complete sentences.   5 4 3 2 1

19. I respect the privacy and confidences of my children.   5 4 3 2 1

20. People listen better when they like what they are hearing. I want my child to listen to me, so I include lots of praise, approval, and encouragement in what I say.   5 4 3 2 1

• • •

TWO HUNDRED AND FIVE WAYS TO PRAISE A CHILD

By using a variety of compliments you will maintain greater credibility and effect when you praise your child. Not only will these expressions enhance your child's self-image, but also the more you use them, the more positively you will see your child's good qualities and achievements.

1. FANTASTIC!
2. THAT'S REALLY NICE.
3. THAT'S CLEVER.
4. YOU'RE RIGHT ON TARGET.
5. THANK YOU!
6. WOW!
7. THAT'S GREAT!
8. VERY CREATIVE.
9. VERY INTERESTING.
10. I LIKE THE WAY YOU'RE WORKING.
11. GOOD THINKING.
12. THAT'S AN INTERESTING WAY OF LOOKING AT IT.
13. IT'S A PLEASURE WHEN YOU WORK LIKE THIS.
14. NOW YOU'VE FIGURED IT OUT.
15. KEEP UP THE GOOD WORK.
16. YOU'VE MADE MY DAY.
17. PERFECT!
18. YOU'RE ON THE BALL TODAY.
19. THIS IS SOMETHING SPECIAL.
20. YOU'RE WORKING SO HARD.
21. THAT'S QUITE AN IMPROVEMENT.
22. MUCH BETTER.
23. KEEP IT UP.
24. THAT'S THE RIGHT WAY.
25. EXACTLY RIGHT.
26. SUPERB!
27. SUPERIOR!
28. GREAT GOING.
29. WHERE HAVE YOU BEEN HIDING ALL THIS TALENT?
30. I KNEW YOU COULD DO IT!
31. YOU'RE REALLY MOVING.
32. GOOD JOB.
33. WHAT NEAT WORK!
34. YOU REALLY OUTDID YOURSELF TODAY.
35. THAT'S A GOOD POINT.
36. THAT'S A VERY GOOD OBSERVATION.
37. THAT'S CERTAINLY ONE WAY OF LOOKING AT IT.
38. THIS KIND OF WORK AND EFFORT PLEASES ME VERY MUCH.
39. CONGRATULATIONS!
40. THAT'S RIGHT. GOOD FOR YOU.
41. TERRIFIC!
42. THAT'S AN INTERESTING POINT OF VIEW.
43. YOU'RE REALLY GOING TO TOWN.
44. YOU'VE GOT IT NOW.
45. NICE GOING.
46. YOU MAKE IT LOOK SO EASY.
47. THIS SHOWS YOU'VE BEEN THINKING.
48. YOU'RE BECOMING AN EXPERT AT THIS.
49. TOP-NOTCH WORK!
50. THIS GETS A FIVE-STAR RATING.

51. BEAUTIFUL!
52. I'M VERY PROUD OF THE WAY YOU WORKED TODAY.
53. EXCELLENT WORK.
54. I APPRECIATE YOUR HELP.
55. VERY GOOD.
56. THE RESULTS WERE WORTH ALL YOUR HARD WORK.
57. YOU'RE A CHAMP.
58. I APPRECIATE YOUR COOPERATION.
59. THANK YOU FOR GETTING RIGHT TO WORK.
60. MARVELOUS!
61. I COMMEND YOU FOR YOUR QUICK THINKING.
62. I LIKE THE WAY YOU'VE HANDLED THIS.
63. WHAT A PERFORMANCE!
64. HOW IMPRESSIVE!
65. YOU'RE ON THE RIGHT TRACK.
66. THIS IS QUITE AN ACCOMPLISHMENT.
67. I LIKE HOW YOU'VE TACKLED THIS.
68. A POWERFUL ARGUMENT.
69. THAT'S COMING ALONG NICELY.
70. YOU'VE SHOWN A LOT OF PATIENCE WITH THIS.
71. IT LOOKS LIKE YOU'VE PUT A LOT OF WORK INTO THIS.
72. YOU'VE PUT IN A FULL DAY TODAY.
73. THIS IS PRIZE-WINNING WORK.
74. A-1 WORK.
75. I LIKE YOUR STYLE.
76. THAT'S VERY PERCEPTIVE.
77. THAT SHOWS A LOT OF SENSITIVITY.
78. THIS REALLY HAS FLAIR.
79. A SPLENDID JOB!
80. YOU'RE RIGHT ON THE MARK.
81. GOOD REASONING.
82. VERY FINE WORK.
83. YOU REALLY SCORED HERE.
84. OUTSTANDING!
85. THIS IS A WINNER!
86. THAT'S A GOOD SOLUTION.
87. YOU REALLY WENT THE LIMIT!
88. FLAWLESS.
89. NOTHING CAN STOP YOU NOW.
90. YOU'RE ONE IN A MILLION.
91. THAT TOOK A LOT OF SKILL.
92. THAT REQUIRED A LOT OF PATIENCE.
93. QUALITY WORK.
94. I WISH I COULD HAVE SEEN YOU DO THAT.
95. SPLENDID!
96. YOU'RE A REAL SUPERSTAR!
97. YOU'VE SURPASSED YOURSELF.
98. THAT'S DANDY!
99. ACES!
100. YOU REALLY KNOCK ME OUT.
101. PRIME WORK.
102. CAPITAL!
103. GRAND.
104. SWELL!
105. NEAT!
106. COOL!
107. OUT OF SIGHT!
108. THAT'S SOMETHING ELSE.
109. NIFTY!

110. WHAT A KEEN EYE YOU HAVE.
111. THAT'S OUT OF THIS WORLD.
112. SOLID!
113. BANG-UP JOB!
114. THAT'S HIGH-CLASS WORK!
115. WONDERFUL.
116. THAT'S FIRST CLASS!
117. YOU'RE IN A CLASS BY YOURSELF.
118. TREMENDOUS!
119. SENSATIONAL!
120. THAT'S INCREDIBLE.
121. THAT'S AS GOOD AS I'VE SEEN!
122. RIGHT ON!
123. WHAT PROGRESS.
124. THAT'S A REAL IMPROVEMENT!
125. YOU'VE COME A LONG WAY.
126. I CAN SEE YOU'VE TAKEN GREAT PAINS WITH THAT.
127. I CAN SEE YOU'VE DONE YOUR BEST WITH THAT.
128. YOU REALLY DID THE BEST YOU KNOW HOW.
129. YOU REALLY APPLIED YOURSELF.
130. I CAN SEE YOU'RE DETERMINED.
131. YOU WERE READY TO TAKE THAT ON.
132. I CAN SEE YOU REALLY STRUGGLED FOR THAT.
133. YOU WENT OUT OF YOUR WAY FOR THAT.
134. YOU PUT YOUR HEART INTO THAT.
135. YOU WENT ALL OUT FOR THAT.
136. YOU SPARED NO EFFORT!
137. I LIKE THE WAY YOU PITCH IN.
138. THAT'S A GOOD WAY TO ATTACK THE PROBLEM.
139. YOU'VE GOT IT IN HAND NOW.
140. HARD JOB, WELL DONE.
141. YOU REALLY KNOW HOW TO HUSTLE.
142. THAT'S VERY EFFECTIVE.
143. YOU MADE SHORT WORK OF THAT.
144. YOU POLISHED THAT OFF.
145. THAT TURNED THE TRICK.
146. THAT DID THE JOB.
147. YOU PULLED IT OFF.
148. YOU CAME THROUGH WHEN YOU HAD TO.
149. YOU DID YOURSELF PROUD.
150. YOU REALLY GO FOR BROKE.
151. THAT'S QUITE MATURE OF YOU.
152. WHAT AN ACHIEVEMENT.
153. YOU'RE A GREAT SUCCESS.
154. WHAT A TRIUMPH!
155. TOUCHDOWN!
156. YOU REACHED YOUR GOAL.
157. YOU HANDLED THAT JUST RIGHT.
158. MASTERFUL!
159. THAT'S A GOOD POINT!
160. YOU RANG THE BELL!
161. YOU REALLY GAVE A GOOD ACCOUNT OF YOURSELF TODAY.
162. YOU DID ALL RIGHT FOR YOURSELF.
163. YOU'RE MAKING HEADWAY.
164. THAT'S A REAL BREAKTHROUGH.

165. YOU CLEARED THAT HURDLE.
166. MADE IT WITH FLYING COLORS.
167. YOU REALLY KNOW HOW TO RISE TO THE OCCASION.
168. YOU KNOW HOW TO PERSEVERE.
169. YOU'RE AHEAD OF THE GAME.
170. SUREFIRE APPROACH.
171. YOU'RE ON A WINNING STREAK.
172. THAT'S VERY RESOURCEFUL.
173. YOU HAVE A TALENT FOR THAT.
174. HIGH-CALIBER WORK.
175. YOU'VE GOT WHAT IT TAKES.
176. YOU'VE GOT THE RIGHT STUFF.
177. YOU'VE GOT A GRIP ON IT NOW.
178. GOOD TECHNIQUE.
179. YOU HAVE A GIFT FOR THAT.
180. YOUR PRACTICE PAID OFF HANDSOMELY.
181. EXPERT!
182. LOOKING GOOD!
183. THAT IS REALLY SHARP.
184. PROFESSIONAL JOB.
185. YOU SHINE AT THAT.
186. YOU REALLY KNOW THAT BACKWARDS AND FORWARDS.
187. THIS SHOWS HOW MUCH YOU CARE.
188. THAT TOOK COURAGE.
189. I LIKE YOUR SPIRIT.
190. I SEE YOU REALLY HAD TO MAKE SOME SACRIFICES FOR THAT.
191. YOU MADE THE RIGHT CHOICE.
192. YOU KNOW HOW TO STAY WITH IT.
193. THAT'S REALLY AMBITIOUS.
194. YOU CAME UP FIGHTING.
195 WAY TO GO!
196. YOU KNOW HOW TO KEEP AT IT.
197. YOU STAYED THE DISTANCE.
198. I LIKE THE WAY YOU FOLLOW THROUGH.
199. THAT'S VERY IMAGINATIVE.
200. HOW EXCITING!
201. TELL ME MORE.
202. YOU'VE GOT MY ATTENTION.
203. YOU'VE GOT MY VOTE.
204. BRAVO!
205. TAKE A BOW.

SELF-IMAGE AND SEXUAL STEREOTYPING

Self-images are based on many elements. These include perceived abilities, actual performance, accomplishments, and other people's opinions. Negative self-images may prevent a child from reaching his potential. One way to reinforce a negative self-image is by sexual stereotyping.

Sexual stereotyping has a long history. Generations of children have been raised on the adage that little girls are sugar and spice and everything nice. Little boys are snakes and snails and puppy dog tails. Girls are encouraged to show emotions; boys are not. In school, girls have long been believed to be more attentive; boys are expected to be disruptive. Girls are thought to play quiet games so they would not get dirty. Boys are told to get "down in the dirt" and compete. Girls are to be protected; boys to be the protectors. These attitudes reflect the tradition, not the reality.

There are real differences between boys and girls. In general, research indicates these differences:

BOYS	*GIRLS*
Are more aggressive	Are more sensitive to taste and touch
Have better daylight vision	Have better night vision
Have math and spatial ability	Have greater verbal ability
Enjoy playing with objects	Enjoy people
Have faster reaction time	Have better hearing
Explore more	Have better manual dexterity

However, research points out tendencies. It does not foretell destinies, and we should not use it to set limits on what our children can do. These real differences do not mean a girl cannot become a mathematician or a boy cannot become an English professor. But statistics show that sexual stereotyping has had real economic consequences:

- Women comprise 51 percent of the work force. However, they earn only $.69 of each $1.00 a man earns.
- In 1983 the median income of female workers was $14,479; the median income of male workers was $22,508.
- Even in fields in which females constitute the majority of workers, the top jobs are held by men. Seventy percent of hospital workers are women; 90 percent of doctors are men. Sixty-seven percent of public school teachers are women, but only 2 percent of secondary school principals and 18 percent of primary school principals are women.

Today's young woman must function in a demanding new economy. The traditional option of getting married and not working after marriage is almost obsolete. "By the time women are middle-aged, we have a 50-50 chance of being divorced, widowed, separated or single. The lesson is perfectly obvious. Women have to take care of themselves," says Jane O'Reilly, a journalist. Considering the increasing number of single-parent homes run by women, a girl today must learn marketable skills. Women need to become more assertive, to be risk takers and decision makers. They need to worry less about being liked and making everyone happy. Fortunately, young girls are seeing more and more successful female role models.

Young boys need love and affection, too. Excessive emphasis on the "macho" image does not help boys grow up to become caring adults capable of sharing their feelings. In an increasingly impersonal and pressured world, caring and sharing are valuable survival skills.

As a parent, you should not discriminate sexually against your child. Your child should be a no-limit person. Today's schools are legally bound to give boys and girls equal chances to excel in athletics, recreation, educational opportunities, and careers. For children to achieve their full potential, schools and parents must work together to combat sexist attitudes in the media, in texts, in other people, and in themselves. Helping your child develop a positive self-image, unbounded by the limits of stereotypes, is an important step in the right direction. A child with a good self-image has greater self-discipline and is more motivated to learn and improve his skills. To improve your child's self-image, believe that your child is the most important child in the world. Then make him believe it!

MOTIVATION

Before a child can be ambitious and successful, he must be motivated. All too often a child who has known failure is quick to say "I don't care" or "I can't" when confronted with any task. The child uses this response to insulate himself from further failure, hurt, ridicule, and lowered self-esteem. For your child to have ambition, he must be motivated to achieve. The way to motivate your child is to let him experience success.

The best motivation is internal. "Do it for Mom or Dad" is not so good as "Do it for yourself." A child is most likely to do something when he wants to accomplish a goal for himself, not because his parents think it is desirable. The problem of internalizing this motivation is that a child who has experienced failure has all too frequently labeled himself as a failure. He believes he is unworthy of success. He may feel unworthy of love and affection.

PARENT ACTION *How You Can Help Motivate Your Child•* The following statements describe everyday situations in which you can contribute to your child's motivation. Rate yourself on each statement by circling the number that best reflects your support. If you score below a 3 on any item, make some changes in that area.

5	4	3	2	1
ALWAYS	VERY OFTEN	SOMETIMES	RARELY	NEVER

1. I help my child set small, short-term, achievable goals that are worded positively: 5 4 3 2 1
   Not—I will not hand in my term paper late.
   But—I will finish my term paper by Friday.
   Not—I will not eat anything fattening until Christmas.
   But—I will lose one pound this week by dieting.

2. I help my child break down tasks into their smallest components.   5 4 3 2 1

3. I show my child that if he is organized, it will be easier for him to be successful.   5 4 3 2 1

4. I help my child link goals to rewards that are relevant to the successful outcome of a task: 5 4 3 2 1
   • *I will finish my term paper by Friday. Then I will spend Saturday afternoon bicycling with Mary.*
   • *I will lose one pound this week by dieting. Then I will buy a new pair of pants.*

5. By my words and actions (body language), I demonstrate faith in my child's abilities to achieve and learn.   5 4 3 2 1

6. I give my child meaningful responsibilities to accept and tasks to complete.   5 4 3 2 1

7. I build my child's self-esteem by immediately reinforcing and praising his attempts at all tasks.   5 4 3 2 1

8. I have high expectations. I assume my child will succeed, not fail.   5 4 3 2 1

9. Once my child begins a task, I do not interrupt him. I am not hasty to correct or im-   5 4 3 2 1

81

prove his methods because he may inter-
pret this advice as criticism and cease trying. I wait for him to enjoy his "success" or
seek my help for improvement.

10. If I see my child making a mistake that will   5   4   3   2   1
    not endanger himself or others, I do not
    prevent him from making it but rather let
    him learn from his failure.

11. Even (and especially) if my child fails, I   5   4   3   2   1
    show caring and love.

12. I discuss with my child specifically why he   5   4   3   2   1
    cannot or will not try something. I do not
    settle for "I don't know." I try to help my
    child express a reason for believing that he
    will fail. Then I can help him cope with
    feelings of inadequacy.

13. If my child is still reluctant or uncertain   5   4   3   2   1
    about how to begin or complete a task, I
    show him a choice of action:
    • *You can either get your school clothes ready for tomorrow or
      get up earlier and look through your closet and dresser in the
      morning.*
    • *You can either do the difficult problems now or get the easy
      questions done first and off your mind.*

14. Any help/advice I offer is geared for suc-   5   4   3   2   1
    cess. If I want to present negative feed-
    back, I sandwich it between praise:
    Positive: You did your homework in record time.
    Negative: You wrote so fast that your writing is hard to read.
    Positive: Your opinions are well-documented by examples.
    Positive: I appreciate the help you gave me with your brother.
    Negative: I wish you wouldn't tease him so much.
    Positive: It was thoughtful to include him in your game.

15. I help my child use language to develop   5   4   3   2   1
    more positive expectations:

• • •

NEGATIVE WORDS	POSITIVE WORDS
I can't	I can
I'll try	I will
I have to	I want to
should have	will do
could have	my goal
someday	today
if only	next time
yes, but	I understand
problem	opportunity
difficult	challenging
stressed	motivated
worried	interested
impossible	possible

The following poem may also motivate your child:

ANYWAY

People are unreasonable, illogical, and self-centered.
  Love them ANYWAY.
If you do good, people will accuse you of selfish, ulterior motives.
  Do good ANYWAY.
If you are successful, you will win false friends and true enemies.
  Succeed ANYWAY.
The good you do today will be forgotten tomorrow.
  Do good ANYWAY.
Honesty and frankness make you vulnerable.
  Be honest and frank ANYWAY.
People favor underdogs but follow only top dogs.
  Fight for some underdogs ANYWAY.
What you spend years building may be destroyed overnight.
  Build ANYWAY.
Give the world the best you have and you'll get kicked in the teeth.
  Give the world the best you've got ANYWAY.

GOAL SETTING

Setting goals is necessary for achieving academic and lifetime success. Goal-setting techniques are key to maintaining a strong self-image and high motivation, as well as fostering the correct expectations for oneself. Goal setting is a skill that should be taught early to a child.

Nine Steps to Successful Goal Setting

1. PLAN for both short- and long-range goals. A goal requires a plan. Help your child determine what changes and skills are necessary for success.
2. BE REALISTIC. Goals should be attainable and worthy of your child's high expectations, good skills, and potential. If goals are too low, your child will not be motivated, satisfied, or challenged to succeed. If goals are too high, your child can become frustrated, lose confidence, or cease trying.
3. BE FLEXIBLE. Your child's goals should be written, not engraved. Let your child know that goals can be modified or expanded. It may be realistic to have a "fallback" position; however, the process of setting goals should not be abandoned.
4. HAVE POSITIVE EXPECTATIONS. All goals should be attainable and reasonable.
5. WORK TOWARD OBJECTIVES. Workable goals consist of a brief series of logical objectives. They should be briefly stated and quite specific. Help your child review the logic of his objectives.
6. SET TIME LIMITS. Specific time limits should be set to achieve goals, so your child can recognize his accomplishments.
7. EVALUATE PROGRESS. To keep your child on target, goals should be reviewed to determine if current behavior matches the desired goals.
8. GIVE ENCOURAGEMENT. Praise completion of actions or goals as it occurs. Emphasize the importance of being conscientious, persevering, and determined.
9. SHARE the attainment of goals with your child and delight in his achievements.

COMPETITION

A strong emphasis on ambition, motivation, and goal setting can result in feelings of competitiveness and stress in your child. Competition can be beneficial, up to a point. Competition can give a child a sense of accomplishment and the feeling that he can excel among his peers in a specific area. But extreme competition often breeds workaholics, critical or self-critical personalities, dissatisfaction, perfectionism, loss of self-confidence, and poor health.

PARENT ACTION *How You Can Help Your Child Develop Healthy Attitudes Toward Competition* • The following statements describe everyday situations in which you can contribute to your child's healthy attitudes about competition. Rate yourself on each statement by circling the number that best reflects your support. If you score below a 3 on any item, make some changes in that area.

5	4	3	2	1
ALWAYS	VERY OFTEN	SOMETIMES	RARELY	NEVER

1. I do not compete with my child. 5 4 3 2 1
2. I do not compare my child to other children or siblings. 5 4 3 2 1
3. I help my child focus on the drive and initiative needed for a task, not the competitive aspects. 5 4 3 2 1
4. I show my child that success is not always measured in terms of beating the competition. 5 4 3 2 1
5. I demonstrate that often one must cooperate with others to achieve success. *Working with others teaches cooperation, leadership skills, problem solving, communications, and conflict management. It also shows a child how his individual ideas and work can contribute to the overall success of a project.* 5 4 3 2 1

VALUES AND RELIGION

"School is not the first to teach values. By the time your child comes to school he has already been educated and miseducated." How good were the good old days for children? In the past, children were appreciated for their economic contribution to their family and society.

- In primitive societies, the young were often prized as the best hunters or gatherers. Young men and women came of age early; life expectancies were brief.
- In the Middle Ages, youths were apprenticed to trades.
- During the Industrial Revolution, child labor was used in the factory and the home.
- In agrarian societies, young people performed many farm chores.

The values children learned were taught in the context of the economic function they fulfilled. They were indoctrinated in attitudes as well as in skills. The world they lived in was the adult world.

Today children are no longer thought of as mere commodities. Instead, their youth is protected and prized. Yet, the values we teach them are often confused. Too often we send mixed messages to each other and our children. While society worships youth in its movies, advertising, and fashions, it also puts youth down. These messages are conflicting, confusing, and difficult for a child (and often for an adult) to understand. Examples:

- You can serve your country in the military, but you can't legally drink at age eighteen in most states.
- Save yourself for sex after marriage; but you can see graphic teenage sex portrayed in movies and on TV.
- I drink and smoke; you shouldn't.
- I take pills for headaches or drink to calm my nerves; but you shouldn't "do drugs."

It is in this kind of environment that the school is charged with the responsibility of teaching values. Values are taught as part of the total educational process—by example, by role models, and in all subjects: math, science, social studies. Values are also implicitly and explicitly expressed in textbooks, by teachers, and in the choice of the curriculum. For that reason, there can be no "value-free" education in school.

Today's schools have a diverse ethnic and religious population. Not everyone wants values taught in school or agrees with the way values are taught. The problem has always been whose values to teach and how to teach them. When schools teach values that differ from a family's own values, there is often conflict. Then the schools lose family support. Recently, the answer has been sought in the courts or legislature in attempts to ban a book or to include a theory in the curriculum. One of the most controversial areas in the teaching of values is religion.

At one time, American schools were closely linked to homogeneous religious communities. A child lived in a one-religion community with the church serving as a religious, social, and cultural focus of the town. To ignore the church was to shun the community. At times, those not participating in religious life were suspect.

The religious composition of this country changed radically with the influx of immigrants with diverse religious backgrounds, and the more recent sprouting of many nontraditional religious institutions. Today, there are more than 160 different religious groups in this country and communities are very diverse in ethnic, cultural, social, religious, and societal values and heritage. Diversity demands that schools as well as communities have greater religious tolerance. Yet, many people want schools to assume some of the tasks that churches or parents have traditionally performed. In many localities, even though the legality of such practices is still in question, schools include prayer, silent meditation, holiday celebrations, graduation service invocations, and holiday assembly programs as part of the educational program.

What is the school's role in a youngster's religious education? Should schools incorporate into their curriculum the teachings that some desire? Whose religion would dominate that curriculum? We believe that the schools cannot and should not teach religion. "The interests of American society are ill-served when they seek to practice their religion where and when it presents an imposition on those of different belief or no belief."

RELIGION IN SCHOOLS

The Supreme Court did not ban all prayer or prohibit academic study of religion. It did rule against the recitation of the Bible for devotional purposes. This is in keeping with the Constitutional dictum that the state or its agent (the school) shall not establish a religion. Here is what schools can legally do:

• Respect the religious preferences of their students by not sponsoring or favoring any one religion over another.

> • Academically study religions. Instruction can include exposure to different types of religions, but not indoctrination. Schools can educate without converting, promoting acceptance, or stressing conformity. Critics suggest that even this dilutes and changes religious teachings. They prefer that courses not be given, if taught on this basis.
> • Emphasize the value of studying religion. Religion has had enormous impact on history and literature; on the development of social institutions; on the understanding of different cultures and values; on the resolution of moral and judicial issues; on all aspects of art, including drama, dance, film, the visual arts, architecture, painting, music, and poetry; on science; and on the promotion of tolerance, as well as the sanctioning of intolerance. To ignore the value and importance of religion's role in history limits our understanding.

The best way to make sure your child is learning the values you cherish is to teach them to him at home. Schools cannot have the same effect or impact on a child as his own family. Values taught in school that conflict with those taught implicitly or explicitly in the home are rarely adopted by a child. The home influence is greater. At best, schools reinforce the values learned at home, but they cannot do this job alone. Nor are teachers and administrators the best people for the job. ". . . make moral education a common cause of parents and the church as well as the school . . . there has been more than enough weakening of the family's ability to provide for itself by a translocation of its core functions . . . to 'professionals' outside the family."

PARENT ACTION *How You Can Help Build Your Child's Values* • The following statements describe everyday situations in which you can help your child learn good values. Rate yourself on each item by circling the number that best reflects your support. If you score below a 3 on any item, make some changes in that area.

• • •

5	4	3	2	1
ALWAYS	VERY OFTEN	SOMETIMES	RARELY	NEVER

1. I respect my child's feelings.   5 4 3 2 1
2. I tell my child how to behave and I set an   5 4 3 2 1
example by my own behavior.
3. I give my child responsibility.   5 4 3 2 1
4. I help my child develop independence by   5 4 3 2 1
giving him opportunities to make choices.
5. I encourage my child to develop a positive   5 4 3 2 1
self-image.
6. We spend time together as a family.   5 4 3 2 1
7. I show caring and compassion for my child   5 4 3 2 1
and for others.
8. I use role playing so I can understand my   5 4 3 2 1
child's point of view and my child can understand mine.
9. I encourage discriminative thinking in my   5 4 3 2 1
child.

Ten Qualities to Build Here is a list of ten qualities that you may
desire your child to develop. Below each quality are examples of
how that quality can be encouraged. As you read each example,
decide whether it is a potential course of action for you. If it is,
place a check next to that idea. Then write down another way you
can build the quality in your child. Using a single strategy once is
not enough. Repetition, reinforcement, and consistency are the
keys to successful development of these qualities in your child.

1. LOVE
——Frequently tell your child aloud, "I love you."
——Love your child even and especially when he does not love
himself.
2. HONESTY
——Choose an appropriate newspaper story or TV program that
deals with violations of honesty. Discuss the repercussions of
those violations in real life and on TV.
——Discuss how honesty has affected the major decisions you've
made in your own life. What has honesty gained for or meant
to you?

3. FAITH
——Build your child's religious foundation by family participation in religious worship.
——Promise your child something he has been wanting or asking you to do—and deliver so he will have faith in you!

4. FAIRNESS
——Ask your child to arbitrate an appropriate family dispute.
——Have your child assign household chores for the family for one week.

5. RESPONSIBILITY
——Give your child a unique and important task to complete this week.
——Have your child plan and complete the family's meals for one night, including shopping, cooking, and serving.

6. COMPASSION
——Show compassion by example: forgive your child when his apology is sincere, so that he will learn forgiveness, too.
——Ask your child to think of some special, unexpected favor he could do for someone—something that would be particularly pleasing to that person—and encourage him to do it.

7. RESPECT
——Teach respect by showing that you are respectful of
  • the environment by not littering
  • traffic laws by not speeding, and
  • other people by treating them politely.
——Teach respect by respecting your child's opinions and privacy.

8. COURAGE
——Encourage your child to express his opinions, even when they're not popular.
——Encourage your child to take karate lessons.

9. EXCELLENCE
——Offer your child a reward for completing schoolwork above his usual competency.
——Ask your child to help another in the area in which he excels. (He will learn excellence by helping another to achieve it.)

10. PATRIOTISM
——Celebrate national holidays by discussing their origin and by not making them just another "day off."
——Teach your child what the freedom of this country has meant to you, your parents, friends, and family.

SUCCESS

The process of developing high expectations in your child takes time and effort. But if you maintain high expectations throughout the school years, your child will achieve more success. If you expect better efforts, you will get better results. For example:

- What would happen if you were told that your child was gifted? Would your expectations change? Would your child's? Most likely you would both have higher expectations of what your child could achieve. The results would be higher achievement even if your child were not really gifted!
- Remember this old gag: Someone is told repeatedly, "You look awful today," until he really begins to feel terrible. What would happen if someone had said, "You look great"?

Negative attitudes can also affect a child's efforts in school:

"You aren't very good at math."

"You are a slow reader."

What would happen if someone said,

"Your studying really paid off; those are the highest marks you have received in that subject this year."

How would your child feel? How would he act? What could he achieve?

Are you helping your child to become successful?

PARENT ACTION *How You Can Use Success Strategies to Help Your Child*
- The following statements describe everyday situations in which you can contribute to your child's success. Rate yourself on each statement by circling the number that best reflects your support. If you score below a 3 on any item, make some changes in that area.

5	4	3	2	1
ALWAYS	VERY OFTEN	SOMETIMES	RARELY	NEVER

1. I help my child create a positive self-image. 5 4 3 2 1

2. I know my child is a winner.   5   4   3   2   1

3. I help my child recognize opportunities for   5   4   3   2   1
achievement by focusing on specific tasks
and setting long- and short-range goals.

4. I do not underestimate or prejudge my   5   4   3   2   1
child's abilities by past performance. If my
child has failed in the past, I help him put
it behind him.

5. I reject labels for my child. I do not think   5   4   3   2   1
of him as "temperamental" or "slow."

6. I expect success and share these expecta-   5   4   3   2   1
tions with my child. I expect and support
my child's "best effort," not perfection.

7. I provide daily opportunities for my child   5   4   3   2   1
to test his abilities and make decisions in
nonthreatening situations. These are opportunities in which he can see himself
succeeding.

8. I encourage practice and repetition of   5   4   3   2   1
skills needed for success, so that when
opportunities arise, my child will be prepared.

9. I praise my child aloud and share his ac-   5   4   3   2   1
complishments with others.

10. I help my child develop incentives—other   5   4   3   2   1
than pleasing me—to perform better. A
child is most successful when he wants to
succeed for himself.

AMBITION, THE WORK ETHIC, AND RESPONSIBILITY

"You must come to [success]. Success doesn't come to you," says
Marva Collins, founder of Chicago's Westside Preparatory School.

One of the qualities that ensures success is ambition. Ambition is
not a bad or "dirty" word. Ambition is often described as a com-
bination of luck and hard work. Those who rely solely on luck discover that it is not enough to ensure success. It is no coincidence
that those who achieve the most, work the hardest. That means
your child must be prepared with the proper skills in order to succeed when an opportunity is presented. A parent cannot make a
child ambitious, but parents can teach their children the signifi-

cance of the work ethic and responsibility. Do not wait until gradu-ation day to teach these concepts. Do not expect the schools or others to do this job. It should be done throughout a child's devel-opment. It can be done in ways that are enjoyable and that add to a child's feelings of self-worth.

PARENT ACTION *The Work Ethic and Responsibility •* The following statements describe everyday situations in which you can instill in your child an understanding of the impor-tance of ambition, the work ethic, and responsibility. Rate yourself on each item by circling the number that best reflects your support. If you score below a 3 on any item, make some changes in that area.

5	4	3	2	1
ALWAYS	VERY OFTEN	SOMETIMES	RARELY	NEVER

1. I encourage my child to envision his contributions to society as positive and im-portant. 5 4 3 2 1

2. I encourage involvement and interest in appropriate part-time jobs, community or volunteer service, political and citizen ac-tion groups. 5 4 3 2 1

3. I demonstrate the importance of working together for a common goal. 5 4 3 2 1

4. I stress the importance of keeping commit-ments. 5 4 3 2 1

5. I stress the importance of setting standards for a performance and striving to meet them. 5 4 3 2 1

6. I point out the rewards (emotional, finan-cial) that I have received for working. 5 4 3 2 1

7. I present a positive attitude toward my own work. I take pride in my achievements. 5 4 3 2 1

8. If possible, I let my child visit me at work so he can see what I do. 5 4 3 2 1

9. I indicate what skills and training are needed to succeed at various kinds of work. 5 4 3 2 1

10. I explain the importance of the work ethic   5   4   3   2   1
    by using examples of family, friends, and
    neighbors. I read to my child about people
    who have been successful in areas that in-
    terest him.

S I X

SETTING LIMITS: WAYS TO IMPROVE YOUR CHILD'S BEHAVIOR

He who spares the rod hates his son, but he who loves him is diligent to discipline him.

PROVERBS 13:24

DISCIPLINE

This Biblical phrase does not mean that a child should be "given the rod." It means a child needs discipline.

To be responsible and independent, children should know there are limits on their behavior and positive or negative consequences to their actions. The "job" of setting limits and meting out consequences is a formidable one. Behavior problems among children today seem complicated because:

Behavior is not monitored as closely as it used to be. In the past, behavior was closely monitored by families, neighborhoods, schools, and religious institutions. "... *everybody supervised everybody's kids. Now a lot of people don't even supervise their own.*"

There is a lack of discipline in the home. Ninety-four percent of

95

teachers and 72 percent of the general public believe this is the major cause of child behavior problems. Not setting limits leads to confusion, game-playing, immaturity, unwillingness to accept responsibility or make decisions, and a lack of self-control. Frequently, this behavior is carried over into the classroom.

The traditional family structure is changing. There are more single parent families in which the demands and responsibilities of parenthood are doubled for that parent. Upheavals in the family structure make misbehavior more frequent and "good" behavior harder to maintain. Too many adults (parents, friends, and family) present poor role models for children.

The United States is a youth-oriented country. Many people believe that too much emphasis is placed on children's wishes, to the detriment of both society and our youth.

A lack of discipline is one of the most important problems facing schools. It is your responsibility as a parent to prepare your child for the classroom by teaching him proper behavior and respect. Support teachers by reinforcing their disciplinary actions. Do not be too hasty to aid and defend your child. Your youngster then will expect you to intervene on his behalf whenever he misbehaves. By "rescuing" your child, you condone poor behavior and encourage disrespect for authority. By setting limits for your child, you teach him how to do that for himself, and enable him eventually to make his own decisions about what limits and which risks are appropriate or sensible for him. Youngsters should be led along a path to prepare them to become self-disciplined and productive citizens. They must respect authority: not fear but honor it. Supportive parents who work with schools are essential for all children to achieve their goals.

Attitudes and feelings cannot be forcibly changed. What can be changed, by using various strategies, are behaviors. Know the difference between an attitude that is displeasing and a behavior that is displeasing. Children are entitled to their own feelings and attitudes. Parents are entitled to see that these attitudes and feelings do not develop into unacceptable behaviors. Developing good behavior in your child takes time, consistency, and praise.

If your child has several behavior problems, do not expect to change them all at once. Initially, target two or three behaviors for improvement. Maintain positive expectations. Focus on the behavior that is wanted, not the one that is to be avoided. Set behavior goals that your child is capable of achieving.

Next, communicate the kind of behavior you desire. Strategies, standards, and consequences of behavior must be communicated to your child before misbehavior occurs. Do not do this in the "heat of the moment." Present the plan to your child when you are calm and not distracted. A good plan includes telling your child:

• How you expect him to behave
• Why it is necessary to change his behavior
• What the consequences and rewards of a behavior change will be
• How his behavior will be monitored

A negative attitude on your part can sabotage any strategy. Avoid:

Questioning .... "Why are you doing that?"
Futile statements .... "You're doing that again!"
Lack of follow-through .... "Don't do that again ..."
The put-down .... "You'll never do it right."
Empty threats .... "If you do that once more, I'll ..."
Unwarranted punishment .... "Do that and I'll really give it to you ..."
Sarcasm .... "You call that room clean?"

A strategy most often fails because it is poorly communicated or it isn't enforced consistently. If a strategy is not working, it may be the wrong one to use. Be prepared to change it to one that is more workable, comfortable, and natural for everyone involved. The same strategy may not work successfully for every behavior change. New strategies may be necessary for new behaviors. Even effective strategies become unnecessary when your child develops self-discipline. That is the goal you are both striving to achieve.

Whatever strategy is selected, you and your child should acknowledge misbehavior when it occurs. Keep in mind that it is the behavior that is unacceptable, not your child. Let your child know that you love him, even and especially when your child does not love himself. Not loving himself may be a source of the behavior problem! Children should feel good about themselves but bad about misbehavior. Your child will behave better if he likes himself.

Both consequences and rewards should be meted out in progressive steps. Once a strategy is set and communicated, the consequences should not be mitigated or changed because of the circumstances. Consistency is the key. Being consistent about consequences will help maintain good behavior. Be predictable in your responses to your child's misbehavior. Be firm and decisive. It is easier for your child to understand limits when the consequences are always predictable. Present the consequences as a choice your child has made by failure to behave properly.

Consequences of misbehavior should follow the action as soon as possible. Do not ignore misbehavior because it is inconvenient to administer consequences at that time. If rules are not enforced daily, your child eventually suffers, and your job as a parent becomes harder. Any strategy requires time, practice, and consistency to achieve results. There are no overnight success stories.

Disciplinary action is used when behavioral standards are not met. The same disciplinary approach may not be effective with all families or all children, at all times or in all situations. Your strategy should be appropriate for your child's age. The strategy should be chosen because it is the one that works best for you and your child.

How to Raise a Juvenile Delinquent in Your Own Family A sheriff's office in Texas once distributed a list of rules under the above title. It is a prescription for what not to do:

1. Begin with infancy to give your child everything he wants. This ensures he will believe that the world owes him a living.
2. Pick up everything your child leaves lying around. This teaches him that he can always throw off responsibility on others.
3. Take his part against neighbors, teachers, policemen. They are all prejudiced against your child. He is a "free spirit" who is never wrong.
4. Finally, prepare yourself for a life of grief. You're going to have it.

The sheriff's office should have distributed the discipline strategies that follow.

A PARENT'S PRAYER

Oh heavenly father, make me a better parent. Help me to understand my children, to listen patiently to what they have to say and to answer all their questions kindly. Keep me from interrupting them, talking back to them, and contradicting them. Make me as courteous to them as I would have them be courteous to me. Give me the courage to confess my sins against my children and ask them forgiveness, when I know that I have done wrong.

May I not vainly hurt the feelings of my children. Forbid that I should laugh at their mistakes, or resort to shame and ridicule as punishment. Let me not tempt a child to lie and steal. So guide me hour by hour that I may demonstrate by all I say and do that honesty produces happiness.

Reduce, I pray, the meanness in me. May I cease to nag; and when I am out of sorts, help me to hold my tongue. Blind me to the little errors of my children and help me to see the good things that they do. Give me a ready word for honest praise.

Help me to treat my children as those of their own age, but let me not exact of them the judgments and conventions of adults. Allow me not to rob them of the opportunity to wait upon themselves, to think, to choose, and to make their own decisions.

Forbid that I should ever punish them for my selfish satisfaction. May I grant them all their wishes that are reasonable and have the courage always to withhold a privilege which I know will do them harm.

Make me so fair and just, so considerate and companionable to my children that they will have genuine esteem for me. Fit me to be loved and imitated by my children. Oh, God, do give me calm and poise and self-control.

Fifteen Discipline Strategies The word discipline is from the Latin *diciplina* which means to teach or instruct. All forms of appropriate discipline should follow this definition and should be designed to instruct. Here are fifteen ways to discipline a child:

1. PUNISHMENT. There are many problems with a discipline strategy that relies primarily on punishment. First

of all, punishment does not show your child how to behave better. It is unpleasant and uneducational. Punishing a child often involves feeling hostile toward him. The effectiveness of punishment decreases with older children, whose attitudes become somewhat blasé and apathetic. Punishment itself may actually reinforce bad behavior if your child perceives it as a way to get attention or to control adult behavior.

Although spanking is the most common form of physical punishment, it is not effective. Spanking does not encourage respect; it builds resentment. When your child is spanked, his mind is not on improving or changing his behavior. He wants to "get even"; he wants revenge. He is learning evasion: he vows next time he "won't get caught." Punishment teaches intimidation and use of force to resolve conflict. (Though a spank on the behind may be effective with younger children to give them a jolt when they've been careless in a dangerous situation, such as running across a busy street.) For parents, spanking can become a simplistic, habit-forming response to their child's misbehavior.

Withholding or taking away possessions has the same negative effects as spanking. This strategy does not focus on changing behavior but on using the weapon of denial as a spiteful deterrent. When this is done excessively, the child learns hatred, hostility, rage, jealousy, greed, shame, and blame. In fact, the denial of an object may have no relationship to the behavior that you want to change: "You didn't fill up the car, so I'm taking away your new album." If possible, punishment strategies should be constructed so that there is a direct relationship between misdeeds and consequences.

2. TIME-OUT. In this method, your child is physically removed from a situation until he can exercise some self-control. He is placed in an area without distractions: a time-out room or corner. Time-out lasts for only a brief period (two to five minutes). Prolonging time-out is counterproductive because it may lead to sulking, along with feelings of guilt, rage, isolation, helplessness, or desertion. Using time-out is most effective with young children.

3. DIVERSION. This is the method in which your child is diverted from the situation that is promoting his misbehavior. Diversion works best with the youngest children. Suggest alternative activities to divert your child from the activity that is contributing to his misbehavior.

4. HINTING. This method is used to defuse a potential situation for misbehaving. Hints are most useful with younger children who may be exhibiting a temporary lapse in a previously corrected behavior. They help your child correct behavior and transform the potential "misbehaving" situation into a learning experience:

- Were you just jumping on the furniture?
- What is the rule about that?
- If you continue to jump on the furniture, what will happen?
- How do you think I feel when you do that?

5. "RULES AND RHYMES" AND "LAYING DOWN THE LAW." The first method is useful with very young children who enjoy learning rhymed rules about behavior. It helps them in a "fun" way to remember how to behave.

Rules for your older child usually mean "laying down the law." Keep rules few and appropriate. Overcontrolling your child's behavior may lead to dependency. Consider your child's abilities, experience, and development. If a behavior is too difficult to achieve in one step, set up goals in increments to help your child attain success on different levels. At each success you will be showing your child that better behavior can be achieved.

6. NATURAL CONSEQUENCES. This method allows your child to suffer through the natural consequences of his action. Parental judgment should be exercised when using this strategy. Examples of natural consequences include:

- After warning your child to be neat when washing, he continues to make a mess in the bathroom. Instead of your cleaning up after him, he gets to mop up the floor and wipe out the sink.

- Your child needs a permission slip signed for school so that he may attend some after-school event. Although you signed the slip a week ago, he keeps forgetting to bring it back to school. The day of the special event he calls you at work and asks you to bring it now. By your not bringing it to him, he misses going to the after-school event because of his own negligence.

7. RESPONSIBILITIES. Help a child behave by giving him appropriate responsibilities. Set your child up for success and build his independence. These responsibilities should be valid and necessary. School should always take precedence over other responsibilities. Do not assign tasks that you hate or that belittle your child.

In completing responsibilities, children may need your supervision or assistance. Here are some responsibilities frequently given to a child:

- Cleaning a disorderly room. Your child may be overwhelmed by this assignment. Use it as an opportunity to help him develop organizational skills. Help him break down the work into tasks. Motivate your child by giving rewards at first. Then encourage him to enjoy the benefits of an orderly room—pride in how it looks and the ability to find things faster.
- Household chores. Problems occur in this area when responsibilities are not assigned fairly or thoughtfully. This causes you to assume an enforcer role when chores are done sloppily. It is a thankless role that discourages responsibility, breeds animosity, and turns every task into a battle of wills.

Problems with chores include:

- *Whose turn?* Even when chores are rotated between siblings, the work may not be divided fairly. Responsibility for a chore can change because of a child's illness, or other important commitments, or swapping with a sibling. Frequent changes can lead to confusion. Many parents have heard:

"It's not my turn."

"I did it last week."

"We traded—she was supposed to do it." Avoid this situation by making changes only when truly necessary. Keep the changes in writing with each child's signature.

• *How hard!* Often children will compare their tasks to those given their siblings. They might think that brother or sister always gets the easier task. Parents will hear:
"She always gets to do that."
"Why do I have to do this?"
You can avoid this in several ways:
Rotate the "fun" tasks.
Have the children help in assigning tasks for that week/month.
Make certain no one task is too time-consuming.

Sometimes when responsibilities are given to a child, he may not want to accept the tasks. Some tactics children use to avoid responsibility are forgetting to complete a task, whining or complaining about it, or doing it poorly. If your child evades responsibility in this way, reassess the task assigned and discuss your child's feelings regarding it. Together you may be able to think of tasks that need to be done and that your child will enjoy doing. These might include watering the plants, washing the car, occasionally going to the market for you, buying the daily newspaper, or getting the mail.

In any event, keep in mind that although a child may not want to do a particular task, it is important for a child to understand that life is made up of tasks and responsibilities that he may not want to do but which are his responsibility to complete in the most effective and efficient manner possible—that is just part of growing up.

8. ROLE PLAYING. Let your child assume your role during an argument. This method defuses emotion from the situation. It gives parents and children insight into each other's thoughts. Role playing can also be quite effective if your child is stubborn.

9. DISCUSSION. Like hinting, this technique enables your child to become more aware of his behavior. When you discuss behavior with your child, point out his positive behavior by using praise. Misbehavior should also be discussed. Use the "Positive-Negative-Positive" principle as a brief reprimand. For example, to a child who quickly cleaned his room, you say:

103

POSITIVE: "You did that very fast. I'm really impressed."

NEGATIVE: "I think if you took a little more time, you could have done it even better."

POSITIVE: "I know I could not have done it any faster."

During discussions you should encourage your child to list any of his behaviors that he sees as problems or sources of anger or frustration. Together analyze which behaviors you both want to change. Limit behavior goals to ensure success. Help him select consequences and rewards to encourage the desired behavior. This strategy works best with the older child who recognizes a behavior that should be changed and is willing to work toward a goal. It requires strong participation and responsibility.

10. FEEDBACK. When your child attempts to improve his behavior, let him know that you support his efforts. Your approach should include these elements:

- Begin by listening to your child. Show rapport, understanding, and acceptance of your child's feelings about his misbehavior. Accepting his feelings does not mean you accept his behavior.
- Review your behavior standards. If appropriate, make your child aware of the reason for these limits and disciplinary consequences.
- Ask your child to paraphrase what is expected of him. Have your child acknowledge that he can control the behavior because he is capable of doing better.

11. PROBLEM SOLVING. In this method, everyone becomes part of the process of setting limits. When parents and children work together for a mutually agreed-upon result, hostility is reduced. To succeed, everyone must make a commitment to the solution. Here are several steps to use:

- Identify the problem.
- Agree to resolve it.
- Have an uninvolved person function as a notetaker during your discussions.
- Brainstorm solutions.
- Hear all viewpoints fairly, without criticism.
- List and review feasible behavior alternatives.
- Agree on a workable (written) solution.

12. CONTRACTS. Parents and children can write a contract to promote good behavior. Elements of a contract include goals and realistic objectives, a time frame, and consequences and rewards. Contracts can be bilateral (both you and your child make promises to perform) or unilateral (you *or* your child makes a promise to perform). An example of a bilateral contract is when a child promises to raise his grade in three subjects and his parent promises to take the child to a professional football game. An example of a unilateral contract is when a child promises to limit his TV watching to weekends.

   As with legally binding contracts, your contract with your child may require an element of compromise. Be willing to negotiate. Both parties should feel that the contract is satisfactory. No one should feel cheated. No one should feel like "the cat who swallowed the canary"! Contracts require a two-way commitment. Upholding the contract teaches maturity, security, trust, responsibility, and delayed gratification. New contracts may be necessary to establish new behaviors.

13. STOP MISBEHAVIOR BEFORE IT BEGINS. Focus on the things your child is doing well now. Prepare a list of his "good actions," and share it with your child. Let him know that you recognize good behavior, improved behavior, and attempts to do better. Be vigilant about catching your child doing something right. Ensure repetition of such behavior by praising your child. Show him that he is a winner. Successful behavior in one area can encourage the same in other areas.

14. REINFORCEMENT. When your child meets his and your expectations, reinforce his behavior. Reinforcement techniques include:

- The most obvious and most neglected verbal response: Say, "Thank you" when your child does what is expected.
- Physical expressions of praise. Give your child a hug.
- Give encouragement. Don't wait until your child finishes a project to praise him. Let him know his preliminary efforts are also appreciated. Validate his self-worth and promote his confidence.
- Praising.
- Sharing your child's successes with others.
- Rewards. Be just as quick to reward as you are to discipline. Intangible rewards include granting special privileges, giving permission to go somewhere, be with someone, or do some special activity. You may allow your child to choose an activity for you to do together such as driving someplace special or attending a sports event or concert. Tangible rewards can include such items as money, clothes, records, or books. Acceptable rewards vary from family to family. These rewards are not bribes. Rewards are given for correct behavior, or close approximations of it in order to encourage success. When you use this technique, make sure your child understands the difference between rights and privileges (the rewards). Ultimately, as behavior remains on target, space out all rewards so that the good behavior itself becomes a reward.

15. PEER PRESSURE. This sometimes negative influence can also work to promote good behavior. For example:

- Enable your child to perceive how his negative behavior is viewed by others. Indicate how the misbehavior affects others, such as fellow students, friends, and family members.

- "Marble Mania" is a game for young children that illustrates the power of peer pressure. In this game, marbles (or any other item such as pennies, plastic figurines, bottle tops, etc.) are an indicator of good behavior. The object is for children to increase their accumulation of marbles daily. Each child is given a different color marble. The child can then track that all the yellow marbles earned that day were ones he received. During the day, a parent schedules when marbles will be rewarded. This is done frequently so that it is unnecessary to keep a list of what a child does to merit the marbles. Marbles are never removed for bad behavior. At the end of the day a count is made of how many marbles were earned by each child. If a child earns enough marbles to meet a previously set goal, a parent may give him a special reward. Group rewards can also be given to all your children when they work together to achieve a specified amount.
- Chart behavior where your child, his brothers and sisters, and peers can see the results. The chart should highlight what was done right, not the misbehavior.
- If your child has a behavior problem, it may be easier for him to correct the behavior by working with siblings or peers who do not have that problem. In this case, peer pressure/sibling pressure can often have a beneficial effect.

PEER PRESSURE AND YOUR CHILD'S BEHAVIOR

Peer pressure and peer relationships are an important part of your child's adolescent experience and behavior. Peer groups have emerged as a major part of the adolescent experience because of the decline of the traditional family. Today's youngster often seeks support and approval from his peer group. Peer relationships are reinforced by the fact that the school day isolates children in groups composed of others their own age.

When they're in a new school situation, students uncannily know, within a short time, the existing "social order" and the groups that comprise it. They know that membership in one clique precludes membership in another. Students dress, act, style their

CHILDREN LEARN WHAT THEY LIVE

If a child lives with criticism,
  He learns to condemn.
If a child lives with hostility,
  He learns to fight.
If a child lives with ridicule,
  He learns to be shy.
If a child lives with shame,
  He learns to feel guilty.
If a child lives with tolerance,
  He learns to be patient.
If a child lives with encouragement,
  He learns confidence.
If a child lives with praise,
  He learns to appreciate.
If a child lives with fairness,
  He learns justice.
If a child lives with security,
  He learns to have faith.
If a child lives with approval,
  He learns to like himself.
If a child lives with acceptance and friendship,
  He learns to find love in the world.

DOROTHY LAW NOLTE

hair, and behave according to the group they wish to join. Cliques reinforce their "uniqueness" by being together at all possible times, treating outsiders as inferior, and defending their group against all others. Peer involvement has positive as well as negative aspects. Peer groups help a child gain self-confidence, assume leadership roles, excel in a given area (for example, a group of peers sharing an interest in computers might push each other to write innovative computer programs), and learn cooperation. These groups also offer support to a child who has problems he is unwilling to discuss with adults.

The Independent Child. Children who are less peer dependent are more centered on themselves. They internalize their own expectations. They are more likely to feel rewarded by accomplishing a task in and of itself than by waiting for approval or recognition from others. But even an independent child will experience a desire for peer approval and acceptance during certain stages.

The Peer-Dependent Child. Membership in a clique gives the peer-dependent child more power. Alone, this youngster may feel inadequate; within a group, he feels more confident. The group allows him to be more assertive. It gives him feelings of belonging, and approval by others. Interestingly, and perhaps not so ironically, peer-dependent children band together and try to emulate independent children. Children who are greatly peer dependent usually:

- Have a more negative view of themselves and of their world.
- Rely on the stimulation of their peers for excitement. Alone, peer-dependent children say they are "bored." They cannot find anything to interest them if left by themselves.
- May be reluctant or fearful to express their feelings to others, especially to parents.
- Do not do as much critical thinking or future planning as more independent children.
- Accept expectations and evaluations of themselves imposed by others.
- Have a strong need for approval.
- Are more fearful of and less assertive about disapproval.

The Wrong Crowd and the Right Crowd. At different times in their adolescence, all children may be members of the "in" crowd or the "out" crowd. Ironically, the two worries most parents have regarding their child and peer pressure are "My child may become involved with the 'wrong crowd,'" and "My child may not be 'admitted' to the 'right crowd.'" It is just as difficult for a parent to get a teenager out of the wrong crowd as it is to get him into the right crowd. Tampering with a situation in some cases may be just as harmful as ignoring it in others. Carefully consider when to take action and when to "stand by." Remember to *give kids enough of the independence they desire so they'll accept the control they need.*

109

PARENT ACTION *How You Can Arm Your Child Against Peer Pressure* • Whether your child belongs to the "wrong" crowd or the "right" crowd, he needs to maintain some independence. You can help him do this. Ten strategies follow:

1. Limit the time spent with the wrong crowd by giving your child extra activities and responsibilities that build self-confidence, such as involvement in a job, sports, or hobbies.
2. Talk about the value of being independent, the importance of having your own ideas.
3. Be involved with your child. Stress how important you are to each other in your family.
4. Keep your child's confidence high. Rejection or disapproval by a group should not diminish your child's self-image.
5. If necessary or possible, remove your child from that class, school, or neighborhood in which peer pressure dominates.
6. If your child is being pressured to act against family standards, help him think of appropriate and acceptable responses to use.
7. Role play with your child to help him cope with his reactions and responses to name-calling, ethnic slurs, and teasing. Tell your child not to underestimate the power of a smile, showing interest, listening, and sharing.
8. Encourage your child to see that he does have choices. Help him act independently by listening to nongroup members. Show him that his independent decisions are as valid as the group's decisions. Discuss the value and importance of dissent.
9. Do not try to break up your child's peer group or confront the children in it. That action may place your child in the position of defending his friends. He will then be driven to maintain even closer ties with them.
10. Explain to your child that everyone copes with peer pressure in some form, even adults. Describe the peer pressure you face from family members, friends, and job associates. Show your child how you handle this pressure.

SEXUAL ISSUES

Just whose responsibility is it to teach children about sex? Parents? The school's? Let's look at some startling statistics:

- By age fifteen, 18.4 percent of teenagers have had intercourse. During ages 15–19 that statistic rises to 42.9 percent.
- At least 2.5 million teenagers will contract a sexually transmitted disease this year.
- The U.S. has the highest rate of teenage pregnancies of all comparable Western nations. By age twenty, one in ten American women has been pregnant at least once.
- Teenaged mothers (aged 19 and under) account for 37.6 percent of all illegitimate births.
- By age nineteen, 28.5 percent of U.S. teenagers who have been pregnant have had a legal abortion.

Our society is a sexually permissive one, sending its messages in many ways. On television, sex is usually portrayed as casual and euphoric; it is the culmination of any relationship between a man and a woman, regardless of their marital status; sexual relationships exist without any of the responsibilities of daily life and without emotional sharing. Other media—for example, song lyrics—reinforce and sanction this perception.

But the media depiction is not the exclusive cause of promiscuity or permissiveness. Adults who have many short-term relationships are also responsible for giving the young people they know unhealthy, unrealistic ideas about sexual relationships.

Sexual cues for teenagers are also set by their peer groups. The prevailing attitude not only questions a girl's right to say "No" but whether it is even wise to do so. Boys frequently approach sex with a "sports" mentality of gamesmanship and scoring. This attitude may now change because of AIDS (Acquired Immune Deficiency Syndrome).

Teaching sexual responsibility should be a parent's job. Parents are best able to provide the moral and religious aspects of educating their children about sex. Yet, when parents do not take the initiative or present this information, it falls to the schools. Many people believe that schools often become hopelessly embroiled in the religious and moral aspects of teaching children about sex.

111

Some people even suggest that the discussion of sexual issues makes sexual experimentation more likely. The Guttmacher Institute, a family planning population institute, contests this belief. Its reports indicate a lower incidence of teenage pregnancy in other Western nations compared to the United States. The Institute believes that the openness of those nations to disseminating sexual information discourages promiscuity.

Sex education, once considered a revolutionary curriculum subject, is now commonly taught at lower and lower grade levels. Such courses are sometimes called "Family Living" or "Marriage Preparation." At other times the information is part of a unit in health or biology. More and more elements have been added to the courses to teach the emotional aspects of sexual experiences as well as the biological information. Many people believe that the schools should reach young adults with accurate information before they become sexually active. That is one of the most powerful reasons why schools are now beginning to incorporate classes or units in AIDS education.

Surgeon General C. Everett Koop states, "We can no longer afford to sidestep frank, open discussion about sexual practices, homosexual and heterosexual. Education about AIDS should start at an early age, so that children can grow up knowing the behaviors to avoid to protect themselves from exposure to AIDS virus." The main focus of AIDS education classes is prevention. Abstinence is clearly the safest choice to avoid sexual transmission of AIDS. Parents most often object when classroom teachers tell students that using condoms can deter the spread of AIDS. Some construe this statement to be an endorsement of sexual promiscuity, sexual activity, or antireligious beliefs. Some parents also object because they do not want the homosexual aspects of the spread of AIDS discussed in class. Nor do they want *any* sexual education discussed in the lower grades. Yet AIDS education, because of the widespread devastating effect of this deadly disease, is rapidly becoming a moral imperative of the schools. Successful teaching of this subject requires time and an understanding of students' needs, problems, and desires. Seventy-five percent of adults favor sex education for high school students; 52 percent of adults support sex education programs on the elementary level. Judging from the popularity, variety, and growing number of these courses, many parents support the school's sex education programs.

You should not rely only on school courses to teach sex education to your child. The family will continue to play a far more critical role than any school or outside agency in setting an example and establishing values for young people, and in providing them with the information they need in order to wisely address issues involving their sexuality. Parents can and should be the primary teachers of sex education. The initial presentation of sexual information is still best done by you. As a parent you are the one to set limits, encourage questioning, and convey values. Schools are best at giving factual information within this framework. Are you helping your child learn about sex?

PARENT ACTION *How You Can Teach Your Child About Sex* • The following statements describe everyday situations in which you can teach your child about sex. Rate yourself on each item by circling the number that best reflects your support. If you score below a 3 on any item, make some changes in that area.

5	4	3	2	1
ALWAYS	VERY OFTEN	SOMETIMES	RARELY	NEVER

1. I share the "facts of life" with my child.   5 4 3 2 1
2. I am teaching my child about sex now instead of waiting until it is too late.   5 4 3 2 1
3. I do not send mixed messages to my child by teaching one kind of behavior and acting another way.   5 4 3 2 1
4. The information I present is not sexist.   5 4 3 2 1
5. I talk about sex in the context of love, responsibility, morality, and maturity.   5 4 3 2 1
6. I use the kind of language my child and I feel comfortable with when discussing sex.   5 4 3 2 1
7. I gear sexual information to my child's needs, interest, and age level.   5 4 3 2 1
8. I do not rely solely on information from books. I present my own feelings and attitudes as well.   5 4 3 2 1
9. I help my child see the importance of setting limits.   5 4 3 2 1
10. If my child has a serious problem regard-   5 4 3 2 1

ing sex, I rely on professional or religious   5 4 3 2 1
counseling as well as our framework of
family values. I try to be sympathetic and
nonjudgmental.

ROLE MODELING

Communicating your values is the key to developing them in your child. And one of the strongest ways to communicate values is by setting an example. Act the way you want your child to act. Consider what values you want to teach and show that you live them daily. To combat the negative influences of the media's presentation of violence, law-breaking, and casual sex, "televise" your own role model. Role modeling can:

- Build compassion and caring in your child.
- Help your child develop a positive attitude.
- Foster significant achievement in language development, reading, speaking, homework, and study habits.
- Help your child to develop a sexual identity and relate to the opposite sex.
- Curtail abusive language.
- Help prevent drug and alcohol abuse.
- Create awareness and concern about dressing and appearance.
- Help your child develop and use good manners.

Good manners are an important aspect of behavior that has been ignored, ridiculed, or demeaned in recent decades. The subject of manners deserves better, and so does society. Manners establish norms for behavior. Manners are social skills. They play an important part in achieving success in society, both socially and economically.

To help your child develop good manners, you do not have to be an authority on etiquette. The "Golden Rule" is the basis for many good manners. Teach your child good manners by your own example. Show your child that being well-mannered has advantages for everyone. A child using good manners shows caring, concern, and an appreciation of others. He gets a good feeling when he makes others feel good about themselves.

The words "please," "thank you," and "sorry" are also part of teaching manners. If you want your child to use these words, you must use them. Most important is the word "sorry." If you want your child to accept apologies from others, as well as from you, you must accept your child's apologies. These are not excuses that imply your child cannot control his behavior in a given situation. Accept sincere apologies and then reaffirm with your child the appropriate behavior goals, strategies, consequences, and rewards.

A Memorandum from Your Child If you're like other parents, you sometimes wonder if you are doing "the right thing" by your child and you hope for direction and comfort. Presented from a young person's perspective, the following points offer insights into the child's expectations of his parents.

1. Don't spoil me. I know quite well I ought not to have all I ask for. I'm only testing you.
2. Don't be afraid to be firm with me. I prefer firmness. It lets me know where I stand.
3. Don't use force with me. It teaches me that power is all that counts. I will respond more readily to being led.
4. Don't be inconsistent. That confuses me and makes me try harder to get away with everything that I can.
5. Don't make promises you may not be able to keep. That will discourage my trust in you.
6. Don't fall for my provocations when I say and do things just to upset you. Then I'll try for more such "victories."
7. Don't be too upset when I say "I hate you." I don't mean it, but I want you to feel sorry for what you have done to me.
8. Don't make me feel smaller than I am. I will make up for it by behaving like a "big shot."
9. Don't do things for me that I can do for myself. It makes me feel like a baby and I may continue to put you in my service.
10. Don't let my "bad habits" get me a lot of your attention. It only encourages me to continue them.
11. Don't correct me in front of people. I'll take much more notice if you talk quietly with me in private.
12. Don't try to discuss my behavior in the heat of conflict. For some reason my hearing is not very good at this time and my cooperation is even worse. It is all right to

take the action required, but let's not talk about it until later.

13. Don't try to preach to me. You may be surprised how well I know what's right and wrong.

14. Don't make me feel that my mistakes are sins. I have to learn to make mistakes without feeling that I am no good.

15. Don't nag. If you do, I shall have to protect myself by appearing deaf.

16. Don't demand explanations for my wrong behavior. I really don't know why I did it.

17. Don't tax my honesty too much. I am easily frightened into telling lies.

18. Don't forget that I love experimenting. I learn from it, so please put up with it.

19. Don't protect me from consequences. I need to learn from experience.

20. Don't take too much notice of my small ailments. I may learn to enjoy poor health if it gets me much attention.

21. Don't put me off when I ask "honest" questions. If you do, you will find that I stop asking and seek my information elsewhere.

22. Don't answer "silly" or meaningless questions. I just want you to keep busy with me.

23. Don't ever think that it is beneath your dignity to apologize to me. An honest apology makes me feel surprisingly warm toward you.

24. Don't ever suggest that you are perfect or infallible. It gives me too much to live up to.

25. Don't worry about how little time we spend together. It is how we spend our time that counts.

26. Don't let my fears arouse your anxiety. Then I will become more afraid. Show me courage.

27. Don't forget that I can't thrive without lots of understanding and encouragement.

28. Treat me the way you treat your friends and I will be your friend, too.

29. Remember I learn more from a model than from a critic.

ADAPTED FROM DR. KEVIN LEMAN'S *PARENTHOOD WITHOUT HASSLES—WELL, ALMOST*, HARVEST HOUSE, 1979, AS QUOTED IN A COLUMN BY ABIGAIL VAN BUREN

SEVEN

THE TROUBLED STUDENT

In today's society the most frightening problems for a parent to confront are a child's failures with school: dropping out, substance abuse, and stress that could lead to attempted suicide. These are just some of the problems associated with a child's failure to achieve in school. In many instances school failure is one of the first signs of more serious problems. The reasons these problems occur are varied and complex. A parent must be observant and sensitive to the signals that indicate a serious problem is developing. Sometimes it is difficult for you to know if your child's problem is caused by a situation at school or at home. To help your child toward success and happiness, it is important to learn the source of the problem.

WHEN YOUR CHILD HAS A PROBLEM AT SCHOOL

From time to time, a youngster experiences problems at school. It's hard not to overreact to your child's complaints, but most often, your child will work his problems out by himself. If his problems continue for longer than two weeks or if he becomes apprehensive about attending school, help him find a workable solution.

To arrive at this solution, there are several steps you should take. First of all you must explore the possibility that your child's unhappiness with school may be caused by a problem at home. Ask yourself if these situations may have affected your child:

• A recent move to a new house or school district.
• Divorce, remarriage, death of a family member.
• Continuous and intense sibling rivalry.
• A change in a family member's health because of illness or injury.
• A change in your work schedule or job that has caused you to spend less quality time at home with your child.
• A change in your child's health.

Your second step should eliminate any peer problems your child may be having. Ask yourself how these situations may be adversely affecting your child:

• A sudden negative change in your child's choice of friends.
• A break-up with a girlfriend or boyfriend.
• Your child's closest friend has moved or changed schools.
• Your child complains his friends ridicule him or do not like him.

If none of these factors appears to be a source of your child's problem at school, review the symptoms your child is having. What type of problem is it?

Attitude:
Is he bored, unhappy, dissatisfied, or fearful?
Does he have behavioral problems in the classroom?
Is he having a conflict with a teacher or some classmates?
Does he skip class, arrive late, or is he chronically absent without an excuse?

Schoolwork related:
Does he have too much or too little homework?
Is he unable to complete the homework in a reasonable time?
Does he always request parental help to do his homework?
Do you or your child disagree with the curriculum content?

Grade related:
Does he think his grades are lower than they should be?
Is he failing or doing poorly in a subject?

Your third step is to visit the school. Call your child's teacher and make an appointment. When you meet with the teacher, ask some general questions:

- What is the subject matter being covered?
- What are the skills he should know?
- What books are being used?
- What type of supplementary material is being used?
- What is the homework policy? What part of the grade does it account for?
- What type of work is done in the classroom? (This may include reading, viewing films, worksheets, class projects in groups or alone, and verbal or written presentations.)
- What is the overall achievement level of the class? (High, average, low, or mixed.)

Ask questions about your child.

- How well does my child get along with his classmates?
- How well does my child get along with you?
- What is my child's strongest subject area?
- What areas are giving my child problems (and how can you help)?
- How is my child doing, compared to his classmates?
- Does my child demonstrate any problems in learning the material?

Be forthright and direct. Carefully explain what problems you believe your child is experiencing. Mention any situations at home that could be having a negative affect on your child's schooling. Ask what situations at school may be causing his problems. Then together you can work on strategies to solve them. If the teacher is unaware that the problem exists, ask to observe the classroom during the school day. Note the following during your observation:

- Is the classroom environment pleasant and stimulating?
- Is the teacher well organized in presenting the subject?
- Are the teacher's directions clear and precise?
- Does the teacher use a variety of materials and techniques?
- Is the class orderly and well-behaved?
- Does the teacher seem to enjoy teaching the students?
- Does the teacher provide time for students' questions?
- Does the teacher encourage each student?

- Does the teacher allow time to work with students individually?
- Does the teacher try to make learning a successful experience for each child?
- Does the teacher use positive reinforcement?
- Is there an undercurrent of hostility? Is your child being teased or harassed, made to feel odd or different?

After your observation, you may decide that your child's problems are school-based. You may learn they stem from the teacher's methods and techniques, or a personality conflict between the teacher and your child. You may decide that this teacher is unable to motivate your child. If any of these are your conclusions, your next step is to try to resolve the problems again by meeting with the teacher.

If you and your child's teacher cannot work out a mutually beneficial solution, make an appointment to meet with the principal. Explain to the principal your specific complaint. Mention the observations you made in the classroom, as well as your talks with the teacher. If you believe that the problem cannot be solved by that teacher, ask the principal to transfer your child to another classroom. It is not necessary to be vindictive or belittling toward the teacher; simply state that you believe transferring your child will allow him to become a better student. Teacher, principal, parent, and child would hope for that as a positive outcome. If your child's problem is not school related you should find appropriate outside counseling and guidance.

FAILURE

Like success, failure follows a spiral path. Failure in one area can breed failure in other areas. The media are constantly affixing blame for failure on the schools. Yet, says Ernest L. Boyer, a noted educator serving on the Carnegie Commission and a former U.S. Commissioner of Education: "The school has little influence over home and the family environment . . . school cannot act in isolation. It cannot solve the dropout problem all alone." Affixing blame does not resolve the problem. If anything, it polarizes the two groups that have to work together to prevent failure—the families and the teachers.

In 1982 there were 26 dropouts for every 100 high school graduates, or about 25 percent nationally. Should the dropout rate be used to measure the effectiveness of schools? Consider the following excerpts from a Mike Royko column, "The Reason for School Dropouts," inspired by the attempted firing of Chicago School Superintendent Ruth Love and the campaign of mayoral candidate Bernard Epton:

Mr. Epton was asked: "If you're elected mayor what are you going to do about keeping our kids from dropping out of school?"

Epton replied: "Nothing. They are your children. It's your responsibility to keep them from dropping out of school."

Royko continues: "Somewhere along the line, many people get the idea that there must be a government service or agency set up to do things for them that they should do themselves.

"The fact is there isn't much that anybody in the school system or in the legislature or in Washington, D.C., can do about the dropout rate.

"One study shows that only 20 percent of Hispanics who start school ever get a high school diploma. If that's true, then I have a suggestion for another study. Interview parents of the 20 percent. Then interview parents of the dropouts.

"I already know what such a study would show. Those who stayed in school probably had someone at home who encouraged them and gave them support. Most of those who dropped out didn't.

"And that's what a study of the dropouts and the graduates of ethnic or racial groups would show.

"Just once I'd like to hear an educator—when some angry parents demand to know why their kids aren't learning—say: "'Look, we don't get them until they're about six. What did you teach them during [the first five] years? And when we do get them, it's only for five hours a day. You have them the other nineteen hours. Now, what have you done? Do you ever go over their homework with them? Do you ever ask them to read for you? Do you ever talk to them about their school work? Do you encourage, reward, stimulate? Do you set up rules? Do you at least turn off the damn TV or the cassette player: That's your job. And if they fail, it's your fault, not ours.'

"So don't point at Ruth Love about the dropout rate. Go look in a mirror."

Frequently, the dropout is seen as a problem only if he is unemployable and a burden to society. And too often, dropping out is accepted as unavoidable among lower socioeconomic groups.

Failure is not a problem just for those parents with failing children. All children are affected by the failure of their peers. Their failure, in school and later in life, affects every child's future.

Failing students are the ones most likely to be truant. As they see it, they have little chance for success in the education system. If that is true, why attend? Why stay in school? The truancy then increases their chances of failure. The attitude and truancy of failing students have an emotional and financial impact on the education of other students. In schools where absenteeism and truancy are high, peer pressure to "cut" may be exerted upon students who regularly attend classes. Constant truancy by a child's peers may cause the child to question the value of staying in school and completing classwork. Truancy costs money. For every student daily attending school, the state gives the school a specific amount of money. When a child is absent for any reason, the aggregate funding that a school receives is reduced. This reduction affects what can be purchased for all the schoolchildren.

25 WARNING SIGNALS THAT A CHILD MAY NEED HELP

1. Low self-esteem
2. Negative attitude
3. Intense jealousy about the birth of a sibling or sibling rivalry
4. Moving to a new home and difficulty adjusting to a new environment
5. Death of a family member or friend
6. Failure in one or more areas
7. Constantly hearing adults or peers devalue education
8. Disruptive home life
9. Inappropriate peers or peer pressure, particularly association with older children or others who have dropped out of school
10. No intellectual stimulation
11. Poor teaching or teaching conditions
12. Poor work or study habits or skills
13. Destructive parental attitudes: domineering, permissive, perfectionist, punitive
14. Entrance into next grade level prematurely despite immaturity or lack of requisite skills

15. Rejection of responsibility
16. Rebellion, impulsiveness, recklessness, resentment of authority
17. Externalization of inner conflicts; hostility
18. Nonparticipation in extracurricular activities
19. Lack of drive or initiative
20. Excessive laziness (using sleep, for instance, to avoid home and school situations)
21. Unrealistic expectations
22. Poor health habits
23. Absenteeism
24. Functional problems, such as poor hearing or vision
25. Cognitive deficiencies; memory or language problems; lack of verbal fluency; inability to master basic academic skills

WHAT TO DO IF YOUR CHILD SHOWS SIGNS OF BECOMING A DROPOUT OR A TRUANT

Many children are exposed to the circumstances that cause failure, yet only some fail. Although the dropout rate peaks in the junior year of high school, the time to prevent failure is not when it is imminent or occurring. By then it is too late. The following methods should be viewed as an "insurance policy" against failure and a prescription for success in school. Not one of these steps works without parental support.

1. Get a commitment from your child to succeed. Ask for his best effort in whatever he attempts.
2. Work with your child's teachers to develop a reward system for class attendance, assignments completed, and so on. An effective system includes rewards for meeting a desired objective, as well as for achieving the ultimate goals. Rewards "along the way" are important motivators. They should be given for sincere efforts and close approximations of desired outcomes.
3. Know the system for making up work due to absences. If your child is so far behind that he believes he will be unable to make up all the missed work, discuss the problem with his teachers. Request that they allow him to show competency for missed work in other ways. Ask

them to let the child "turn over a new leaf" and be judged on his work and effort from this moment on.

4. Seek professional guidance and counseling from the school. The methods and therapies schools use include:
   - Providing your child with a glimpse of the future. He visits the next grade level to learn what is expected and what can be achieved.
   - Exposing him to the real world. Your child visits with past dropouts who are attempting to overcome their academic deficiencies.
   - Setting a specific goal for your child that is focused on changing behavior first, then attitude.
   - Considering options for special schools or magnet schools that have alternative education programs. These offer a wider variety of courses structured within a nontraditional framework.
   - Attending work co-op programs or tutoring sessions.
   - Involving your child in extracurricular activities or nonschool experiences where he can achieve success and recognition.
   - Helping your child build a relationship with other adults (teachers, friends, or relatives) who can be role models and nurture his desire for success.

5. Use of mastery learning. This is a concept of learning based on the observation that all children learn at different rates, at different times, and in different ways. If each child could be instructed in the best way and at the best time and speed for himself, he could master the required learning. It has been thought by leading educators such as Theodore R. Sizer, of Brown University, that this type of program might reduce the failure rate for students. Studies by Benjamin Bloom of the University of Chicago reveal that as many as 90 percent of the students can learn these school subjects up to the same standard that only the top 10 percent of students have been learning under usual conditions. The basic techniques of mastery instruction include:

   - Statement of objectives
   - Brief learning units
   - Testing

- Giving cues
- Reinforcement
- Student participation
- Giving corrective feedback

Schools with mastery learning programs group students by their ability to master the subject, not by age or class. Mastery of a subject determines when a student will progress to the next level of learning. The benefits of mastery learning for a child include:

- More time-on-task to master and complete units of study.
- Time to do more independent projects.
- Greater self-awareness of accomplishments and skills.
- Higher expectations.
- Increased self-confidence and a better self-image.
- Development of a successful and enjoyable pattern for learning.

6. Help your child focus on areas where success can be realized. When he experiences success in a particular subject, he will begin to like it better and work harder. Success in one area breeds success in other areas.

Repeated success in school over a number of years increases the probability of the student's gaining a positive view of himself and an ability to withstand stress and anxiety more effectively than individuals who have a history of repeated failure or low marks in school. Repeated success in coping with the academic demands of the school also appears to confer upon a high proportion of such students a type of immunization against emotional illness. Similarly, there is evidence that repeated failure or low performance in school increases the probability of the student's developing a negative view of himself and contributes to emotional difficulties and mental illness.

7. Catch your child doing something well and praise him. Ironically, those in greatest need of high academic marks as motivation are the ones least likely to receive them. Do not wait for your youngster to achieve that "A." Do not wait for some momentous achievement to occur. Acknowledge daily your child's small successes.

8. Be involved in and committed to your child's schooling. You should know what is expected of him academically. Know what standards he has to meet. Know his schedule and his teachers. If your child is failing:
   - Early intervention is essential. Do not accept failure as inevitable and do not let your child accept it as such either.
   - Do not let poor past performance eclipse future potential.
   - Do not equate mistakes with total failure. Do not let your child do so, either.
   - View failure as a choice, a poor but correctable decision made by your child, and help him understand how he can learn to improve from it.
   - Make your child aware of where he stands. Let him neither ignore his failure nor hide from it.
   - Motivate your child. Link learning to future successes and opportunities.
   - Discuss, with the teacher and your child, how far he needs to go to become successful. Discuss what skills he will need in order to succeed.
   - Explain how you as a parent, along with the teacher, will help him to succeed.
   - Show your child how he can be become successful. Discuss success objectives in increments. Explain what will be required of him.
   - Be supportive—praise and appreciate your child. Help him build higher expectations.
9. Improve your child's health habits. Make sure that he is physically fit to learn by being well nourished and well rested. Other aspects of being fit to learn may include participating in exercise or athletic programs. Don't neglect routine medical and dental check-ups.
10. Stress the importance and responsibility of getting a good education. Explain how your education has helped you. Children should be aware that they, too, are responsible for what they learn and achieve.

"Many students find little incentive in hard academic work. Although they want their diplomas, they earn them primarily by doggedly dutiful attendance rather than by an exhibition of mastery of the substance of study. Thus there is little need to suffer the pain of stretching one's mind. Students are rarely expected to educate themselves. They are 'delivered a service.' . . . For all too many, school is an entitlement and thus, curiously, is not respected as much as those activities [such as sports or music] that require adolescents to make a significant personal investment."

SUBSTANCE ABUSE

It has been said that the greatest threat to our country is the abuse of drugs by all facets of our society. The school is but a microcosm of society at large. In order to reduce the chemical abuse among our student population we must also effectively deal with the larger issue of drugs in society. The statistics about drug and alcohol abuse among teenagers are alarming.

Drinking Statistics
- *Three million* teenagers between 14 and 17 have a drinking problem.
- One-third of all high school students get drunk once a month.
- Four out of ten people killed in drunk driving accidents are teens.
- Accidents resulting from drunk driving are the #1 killer of children in this country.
- Five percent of high school students use alcohol daily.

Drug Statistics
- Eighty-five percent of children over ten years of age experiment with drugs.
- A recent National Institute on Drug Abuse survey reported that 57 percent of all high school seniors have tried stimulants, and 16 percent have used cocaine.
- Six percent of high school students use cocaine. That figure has tripled since 1975.
- Five percent of high school students use marijuana daily.
- "The importation and sale of cocaine is the sixth largest business in the United States. Marijuana is the fourth largest agricultural crop in this country."

These statistics are significant for all parents. Can any parent guarantee that his child will not be involved in some type of substance abuse? Most parents cannot answer with an unqualified "yes." All children are at risk. Preventive measures and attitudes are essential. Although many schools have programs addressing the problems of abuse, your role as a parent is to be knowledgeable, to communicate with your child, and to take action when necessary.

PARENT ACTION *How You Can Help Prevent Alcohol and Drug Abuse •* The following statements describe everyday situations in which you can help protect your child from drug and alcohol abuse. Rate yourself on each item by circling the number that best reflects your support. If you score below a 3 on any item, make some changes in that area.

5	4	3	2	1
ALWAYS	VERY OFTEN	SOMETIMES	RARELY	NEVER

1. I constantly build my child's self-esteem. 5 4 3 2 1
2. I take time to love and be with my child. 5 4 3 2 1
3. I have patience for my child. 5 4 3 2 1
4. I get the facts and educate myself and my child to combat the sometimes alluring, "fun" image of alcohol and drugs portrayed by the media and peer groups. I indicate how substance abuse can negatively affect the lives of others. 5 4 3 2 1
5. I set an example by not "doing" drugs. I limit my own use of alcoholic beverages and over-the-counter or prescription drugs. 5 4 3 2 1
6. I know my child's friends. I tell my child that if friends are "pushing" drugs or drinking, they are *not* friends. They are out to hurt themselves and him in the process. I help my child develop the courage to hold onto his convictions and to leave these friends. 5 4 3 2 1
7. I keep my child involved in family life. 5 4 3 2 1
8. I communicate with my child. I listen to him. I tell him that drinking and taking 5 4 3 2 1

drugs are a way of avoiding problems and   5   4   3   2   1
that they only make them worse and create
new problems of dependency.
9. I stress the cost of substance abuse upon   5   4   3   2   1
the emotional and physical well-being of
children and all family members.
10. I indicate how substance abuse can de-   5   4   3   2   1
velop into an uncontrollable addiction.

**WARNING SIGNALS THAT YOUR CHILD MAY BE
ABUSING ALCOHOL OR DRUGS**

• **Lack of communication: avoiding conversation, memory loss, inability to concentrate or understand, secretive phone calls.**
• **Decrease in family interaction: keeping to one's room, spending longer periods of time with "new" friends who may be older, "cool," sloppy, or secretive.**
• **More criticism of your lifestyle and increased sensitivity to all your demands. Disrespectful, abusive language.**
• **Immaturity, apathy, lethargy, lack of motivation.**
• **Physical evidence: drug paraphernalia, extensive use of eye drops. A child abusing drugs or alcohol may be accident-prone, sensitive to light, frequently sick with respiratory or skin ailments.**
• **Increased need for money (for drugs) or increased income (from drugs).**

Seven Steps to Help Your Child Overcome Substance Abuse If
your child is already a drug or alcohol "statistic," here are some
steps to take:

1. Do not panic. If you are to help your child, you must be
   able to make thoughtful decisions.
2. Do not feel that you are the victim—your child is the one
   who needs immediate help.
3. Do not ignore the problem any longer. Confront your
   child with his abuse problem. The only person who can
   stop your child from substance abuse is your child. The
   first step is for him to make that commitment to himself.

Keep the lines of love and communication open. Let your child know that you hate the alcohol or drugs but that you love him.

4. Make it clear to your child that you will do everything within your power to stop his abuse. You will strictly monitor all activities and friends; alert friends' parents and teachers; deny him car privileges and money; inspect his room; and have him account for his time.

5. Be willing to make and live by some hard decisions: this is called "tough love." It is a strategy by which parents sometimes take radical actions to control abusive behavior, harmful to the child and others, for the child's benefit. Actions may include enrollment in residential programs, calling in the police, or barring a child from the home until certain behavior criteria are met. You and your family should be prepared to make a strong, consistent commitment to your child. Seek support from other "tough love" families and professional counselors.

6. If appropriate, get expert counseling. Programs include peer-counseling and counseling with trained ex-abusers, as well as with traditional professionals. Whatever program is selected, it should be well-documented and supervised.

7. Get support for yourself and other family members, as well as for the abusing child. Find a counselor, clergyman, or group who can communicate with your family and who will take a sincere interest in your child.

STRESS

Stress in itself isn't bad; it's how one reacts to it. Some children can thrive on moderate amounts of stress. They may need that extra parental push to reach peak performance. These children see stressful events and situations as challenges and obstacles to overcome.

Unfortunately, like adults, not all children do well in stressful situations. In the school-aged child, stress can be caused by factors at home or at school.

School situations that induce stress include:

• Poor relationships with peers leading to feelings of inadequacy.

- Peer pressure that a child doesn't know how to handle.
- Breaking up with a boyfriend or girlfriend.
- Sudden success in school leading to expectations of continued success.
- Failure in school that a child perceives as insurmountable.
- Changing schools or being promoted early to the next grade.
- School tests.
- Reports and homework.
- School vacations and holidays that separate the child from his peers.

Home situations that induce stress include:

- Change in family structure such as divorce or remarriage.
- Family member's death, illness, or injury.
- Ongoing or unexpected family economic problems.
- Birth of a sibling.
- Poor family relationships.
- Pressure to achieve from family members.
- Moving to a different neighborhood.

The stressed child exhibits a variety of symptoms, but basically a child will try to cope with stress in two different ways: flight or fight. The child who uses the flight mechanism of coping generally will internalize the stress. If your child does this he may have a variety of physical symptoms such as headaches, stomachaches, poor eating habits, lack of attention to grooming, frequent illnesses, weight loss, hyperactivity, breathing problems, muscle tension, lack of sleep, or excessive sleepiness. His stress problems are having the greatest observable impact on himself. He copes by using illnesses and ailments to excuse himself from stressful situations.

The child who uses the fight mechanism of coping generally will externalize the stress. If your child does this he may exhibit symptoms such as frequent crying, nervousness, a short temper, hostility, moodiness, uncooperative behavior, pessimism, uncommunicativeness, whining, complaining, lack of humor, and extreme sensitivity. His stress reactions are having the greatest impact on his relationships with others. The fact that these relationships are becoming negative exacerbates his stress.

Both fight and flight types of behaviors can exist simultaneously in a child. If your child is in a stressful situation, you generally cannot control the cause of the stress. What you can do is help your child find healthier ways of reacting to stress.

PARENT ACTION *How You Can Help Your Child Cope with Stress* • The following statements describe how you can help your child use beneficial stress reducers. Rate yourself on each statement by circling the number that best reflects your support. If you score below a 3 on any item, make some changes in that area.

5	4	3	2	1
ALWAYS	VERY OFTEN	SOMETIMES	RARELY	NEVER

1. I encourage my child to talk to me about his fears and anxieties.   5 4 3 2 1

2. If I think my child is pushing himself too hard, I tell him it's all right to slow down, cut back, or stop to smell the roses.   5 4 3 2 1

3. I discuss with my child stressful situations I have experienced, and how I have learned to cope with them.   5 4 3 2 1

4. I help my child use imagery to reduce stress. (He learns to think of a restful scene or happy event until he regains the self-control to deal with a given situation.)   5 4 3 2 1

5. My child and I practice relaxation techniques such as meditation and deep breathing exercises.   5 4 3 2 1

6. I encourage my child to make his room into an environment where he can relax and reduce stress through his favorite music, color, and art.   5 4 3 2 1

7. I encourage my child in daily stress-reducing activities that he can do at home.   5 4 3 2 1
These may include hobbies, dancing, singing, caring for a pet, and reading.   5 4 3 2 1

8. Laughter is often the best medicine. My child and I share fun times and jokes together. We take time to be silly.   5 4 3 2 1

9. I encourage my child to participate in physical activity or sports to reduce stress. This can include regular exercise and walking.   5 4 3 2 1

10. I sometimes adhere to that ancient adage —"when the going gets tough, the tough go shopping," especially if it can reduce stress in my child.   5 4 3 2 1

11. I allow moderate television and video game playing to reduce my child's stress.   5 4 3 2 1

12. Sometimes old remedies do work. If I think my child had a difficult day, I suggest a warm bath, relaxing shower, or even provide cookies and milk!   5 4 3 2 1

13. I help my child organize and prioritize his time so he does not panic when a homework assignment is due.   5 4 3 2 1

14. If my child experiences stress when taking tests at school, I help him prepare for them.   5 4 3 2 1

15. I provide nourishing meals for my child and emphasize the importance of maintaining one's strength and health to cope with difficult problems.   5 4 3 2 1

16. Together, we try to anticipate situations that will cause my child stress and develop positive ways to handle his reactions.   5 4 3 2 1

SUICIDE

Children who are deeply affected and harmed by stress can become very apprehensive and frustrated and may experience significant emotional as well as physical pain. Serious stress-related symptoms include a sudden change in behavior, unwillingness to communicate, nervousness, belligerence, and "escaping" (sometimes by substance abuse or isolation).

Basically, what young people who attempt suicide share in common is a belief that they have no options or control over their lives.

The following signals, based on statistics from the National Center for Health, should prompt parents to seek psychological or psychiatric help for their child and the family:

TEN SUICIDE WARNING SIGNALS

1. Preoccupation with themes of death or expressing suicidal thoughts.
2. Giving away prized possessions; making a will or other final arrangements.
3. Changes in sleeping patterns—too much or too little.
4. Sudden and extreme changes in eating habits; losing or gaining weight.
5. Withdrawal from friends and family or other major behavior changes.
6. Changes in school performance (lowered grades, cutting classes, dropping out of activities).
7. Personality changes such as nervousness, outbursts of anger, or apathy about appearance and health.
8. Use of drugs or alcohol.
9. Recent suicide of friend or relative.
10. Previous suicide attempt.

Most parents will never have to deal with this problem. However, it is important that these warning signs in adolescents be taken seriously. Suicide threats should not be taken lightly, even if they seem to be impulsive statements made during a quarrel. Parents should seek competent professional help quickly.

THE TIME IT TAKES
TO LEARN:
UNDERSTANDING THE
SCHOOL DAY

I n a typical classroom, a teacher often devotes time to non-teaching tasks. These administrative functions include taking attendance, disciplining students, collecting or returning material, and making announcements. The time the teacher devotes to instructing students in academic subject matter is called time-on-task. It is the class time during which a student is actively engaged in learning. It is the time spent on reading, writing, study, instruction, reinforcement, homework review, and responding to questions.

Time-on-task is also shortened by the length of the school year. In most states the school year is 180 days long. Although high school students attend school about five to six hours per day, five days a week, nine months per year, academic learning is not occurring every hour of the school year. Professional educators who conducted classroom observations of high school students report that students may spend as little as two to four hours per day on academic instruction.

Time-on-task for academic instruction has also been lost because of the changing school curriculum. In the past fifteen years there has been growth in the non-academic area of the curriculum indicated by the addition of courses in physical education, band, orchestra, driver education, cooperative education (work/study programs), health, shop, home economics, and family living. The time that a student spends in these subjects reduces the time he could be using to take more academic course work. Although the course offerings in school have expanded, the time a student has to complete all these courses has not grown in proportion; neither has the money to develop programs, recruit teachers, and equip classrooms for implementing the programs.

The loss of time-on-task in the classroom is a serious problem for students and teachers. Time is allocated for lunch, recess, assemblies, changing classes, and homeroom exercises. These tasks can amount to an average loss of 16 percent of instructional time. Time-on-task is also decreased by students' skipping or cutting classes, illnesses, socializing, doodling, and daydreaming. About ten days (11 percent) of designated instructional time is lost to student absenteeism. In the *average elementary school* situation, ". . . the school year is 180 days, with students attending 160 days. Each school day of about 5 hours includes about 2 hours of reading/language arts instruction and about 45 minutes of math instruction. Students are engaged [time-on-task] about 60 percent of the allocated time, spending about 72 minutes on task for reading/language arts and about 27 minutes on task for math. They are working successfully on relevant academic tasks for about half this time, about 36 minutes each day for reading/language arts and 14 minutes each day for math. During an average school year, students thus have about 96 hours of academic learning time in reading/language arts and about 37 hours in math."

The following chart shows how time is spent in an average elementary school. The next charts indicate time-on-task in two hypothetical elementary schools: one with a lower and one with a higher average number of attendance days in the school year.

• • •

DAILY CHARTS OF TIME-ON-TASK
IN ELEMENTARY SCHOOLS

AVERAGE TIME-ON-TASK (QUALITY LEARNING TIME)
(based on a 5-hour day for 160 days)

TIME	READING	MATH
Allocated	120 minutes	45 minutes
Engaged time-on-task	72 minutes	27 minutes
Focused academic learning	36 minutes	14 minutes
(50% of engaged time)		
Yearly academic learning time	96 HOURS	37 HOURS

LOW TIME-ON-TASK
(based on a 4.5-hour day for 150 days)

TIME	READING	MATH
Allocated	90 minutes	30 minutes
Engaged time-on-task	41 minutes	14 minutes
Focused academic learning	12 minutes	4 minutes
(30% of engaged time)		
Yearly academic learning time	30 HOURS	10 HOURS

HIGH TIME-ON-TASK
(based on a 5.5-hour day for 170 days)

TIME	READING	MATH
Allocated	150 minutes	60 minutes
Engaged time-on-task	113 minutes	45 minutes
Focused academic learning	79 minutes	32 minutes
(70% of engaged time)		
Yearly academic learning time	224 HOURS	90 HOURS

The problem of time-on-task learning is more complex at the secondary school level. On the average, high school teachers teach five to six classes per day. They devote an average of fifty-four minutes of time in school to preparing for these classes. Much of that time is used to review lessons, grade papers, complete report cards, and counsel. This work is usually done under difficult circumstances: Traditionally, teachers are not given their own workplaces with desks, offices, or phones. Other duties assigned during the day (lunchroom duty, hallway patrol, chaperoning, checking passes or IDs, and attendance reporting) also interfere with teaching time.

During the school day, there are some activities and events that may interfere with your child's academic time-on-task. Events can include sports assemblies, band or orchestra performances, an assembly hosted by a visitor (such as the police, the PTA, the military), the yearbook committee, or a holiday program. School activities might include decorating the gym for a dance, playing host to potential students coming from other schools, setting up the cafeteria as an auditorium for an upcoming event, or serving as aides to teachers by preparing material. Many students enjoy these events and activities and give more of their time to them than they do to academics.

"Two hundred years of affluence have enabled the U.S. to take on every society task, tackle every social ill, try to solve every national problem by means of the public schools. Various forces in society seek to get their special interests legitimated in educational goals and school programs. What are predominately economic, political or social goals take on an educational veneer." Today's schools are asked to give children more than academic knowledge and skill. They are called upon to teach religious tolerance, the work ethic, morality, and values as well as to facilitate upward mobility, end racial prejudice, and eradicate sexism. Frequently, medical, psychological, social welfare, and child protective agencies use school time to test students. All these programs are perceived as benefits for your child. While they may be beneficial, they do have a price. Education is not "free" when adding to the non-academic curriculum means constantly expanding costs. Attempts to solve social problems within the school curriculum are shown in the following chart:

• • •

PROBLEM	CURRICULUM SOLUTION
Venereal disease	Sex education
Driver safety	Driver education
Poor physical health of youth	Physical education
Assimilation of immigrants	Bilingual education
Unemployment	Vocational education
Substance abuse	Alcohol/drug education
Disintegration of traditional family	Marriage/family courses
Decline of work ethic	Work co-op programs
Technological illiteracy	Computer courses
Environmental problems	Environmental studies
Minority discrimination	Cultural appreciation and political science
Political instability	U.S. government and law
Sexual inequality	Feminist studies

As educational tasks multiply, a school that is asked to do them all finds it very difficult, if not impossible, to maintain a clear sense of mission.

It is difficult to allot enough time-on-task for academics. Before any subjects are added to the school's curriculum, parents should ask schools these five questions:

1. Can a group other than the school assume this responsibility more effectively?
2. Is this part of the school's academic mission?
3. Can the school still accomplish its academic goals?
4. Is the child really being served?
5. Does the school have the time, money, and staff to do this task effectively?

WHAT SCHOOLS DO BESIDES TEACH ACADEMIC SUBJECTS: EIGHTY-FIVE REASONS FOR LOSING TIME-ON-TASK

HEALTH-RELATED PROGRAMS

1. General physicals
2. Testing for vision
3. Testing for hearing
4. Sickle cell anemia screening
5. Scoliosis screening
6. Dental care and check-ups, fluoride programs

7. Immunizations
8. Poison control and prevention
9. AIDS education
10. CPR
11. Checking for lice and scabies
12. Sex education
13. Pregnancy counseling and prenatal care
14. Drug abuse programs
15. Alcohol abuse programs
16. Tobacco abuse programs
17. Reporting and counseling of child-abuse victims

FIELD TRIPS

18. Educational
19. Recreational

SAFETY-RELATED PROGRAMS

20. Traffic safety, including driver education
21. Bus safety drills
22. Bike safety drills
23. Fingerprinting
24. Theft and vandalism prevention, including teaching the consequences of shoplifting
25. Firearms safety
26. Juvenile law and criminal justice
27. Crime prevention-defensive training programs
28. Fire drills
29. LUNCH AND BREAKFAST PROGRAMS
    These are big business. The public schools comprise the fourth largest food service industry in the United States. Only McDonald's, Burger King, and Marriott are larger. Of the 42 million students attending school, 23 million eat school lunches.
30. LATCHKEY PROGRAMS/DAY CARE/ SUPERVISED AFTER-SCHOOL PLAY
31. TRANSPORTATION
    Besides transporting students between home and school, schools frequently provide transportation to after-school events.
32. INSURANCE, including costs for student accident policies.
33. SOCIALIZATION PROGRAMS for the elimination of racism and sexism.

34. RECRUITMENT by military services, youth groups, and so on.
35. CHARITY DRIVES
36. CONTESTS

ADMINISTERING TESTING PROGRAMS

37. College admission tests
38. Scholarship testing
39. Statewide comparison/achievement tests

HOLIDAYS

40. Schoolwide holiday celebrations
41. Special recognition days
42. ILLNESS/ABSENTEEISM of teachers and students

ASSEMBLIES

43. Academic awards
44. Sports awards
45. Films
46. Speakers
47. Musical programs
48. Plays

SPECIAL EVENTS DAYS

49. Barbecues
50. Sports/homecoming rallies
51. Parades

PROGRAMS COMPETING FOR ACADEMIC TIME
AND RESOURCES

52. Education of children of migrant workers
53. Bilingual and ESL (English as a Second Language)
54. Special Education
55. Services such as Chapter I programs that "pull" students out of academic class for remedial reading, math, and speech
56. Guidance
57. Career education and information
58. Discipline

STUDENT VOLUNTEER SERVICES

59. Library
60. Hall monitor
61. Athletic program assistant
62. Cafeteria monitor
63. Study hall monitor
64. VOLUNTEER/COMMUNITY SERVICE

(According to a 1984 Gallup Poll, 79 percent of the public would like students to have the opportunity to earn credit for this type of work.)

65. WORK/CO-OP PROGRAMS: STUDENT ACTIVITIES DURING THE SCHOOL DAY
66. Student government
67. Assemblies
68. Concerts and performances
69. Committee meetings
70. REHEARSALS for school plays, musical assemblies, band, chorus, and so on.

TEAM AND INDIVIDUAL SPORTS

These are important in teaching competition, leadership, self-confidence, and self-image, but athletics can interfere with academic time-on-task.

71. Practice
72. Actual game time
73. Cheerleading practice and pep rallies
74. Transportation time back and forth to events

CLUBS

75. Social clubs
76. Vocational clubs
77. Shared-interest clubs
78. Academic clubs
79. Newspaper

END-OF-YEAR EVENT PLANNING

80. Yearbook
81. Senior trips and picnics
82. Senior pictures
83. Senior rings
84. Graduation rehearsal
85. Proms

While the above items do take away from "time-on-task," many of these activities are important and necessary for a healthy well-rounded school program and community. Since the elimination of many of these activities is not a viable possibility, we must look for other ways of increasing "time-on-task" or utilizing outside agencies.

TEN WAYS TO IMPROVE TIME-ON-TASK IN SCHOOL

1. INCREASE THE TOTAL AMOUNT OF TIME SPENT IN SCHOOL BY LENGTHENING THE

SCHOOL YEAR. The current school year is still geared to an agrarian society. When our nation had a farm economy, youngsters were needed for farm chores during summer months. They could easily find work helping out on the farm. Today, those seeking summer employment usually have a difficult time finding a financially or personally rewarding summer job.

A longer school year correlates with higher achievement. The more time a child spends in school on academic subjects, the more likely his success in those areas. It has been shown that high achievers spend more time in school than low achievers. This is not surprising because high achievers associate school with positive feelings about themselves. They are rewarded with good grades. Conversely, low achievers do not desire to invest more time in a system that they believe is unlikely to reward them for their effort. Ironically, they are the ones who could benefit most!

If a longer school year is to be successful for both high and low achievers, it must be supported by the public and the educational staff. Yet, a longer school year is opposed by 50 percent of the public, even though research conclusions show that it would be beneficial. For a longer school year to succeed, the public must support it. Taxpayers would need to assume more of the financial burden of increased operating costs. Lastly, educators would need to develop an enriched curriculum that would creatively utilize this extra time-on-task for learning.

Children do not need a break from school. They do not burn out. More often it is the parents who want a break from school because they have plans to take their children on a summer vacation, send them to camp, visit relatives, travel, and so on. There is nothing wrong in this.

But schools can easily go full time on a yearly calendar with a 3-week break scheduled quarterly. This is being done in some schools with success. Demand for daycare/latchkey programs through the summer months may increase as more families need income from both parents. Why not utilize that time to teach?

2. INCREASE THE TOTAL HOURS SPENT PER DAY IN SCHOOL. Proponents for increasing the amount of time spent in school argue that it would allow more learning to occur. It would also maximize use of facilities throughout the school day and year. Schools and communities would have to be prepared to compensate teachers economically for this new time structure. We believe this investment in students is worth the time and money.

Objections to this strategy include the fact that it infringes upon after-school activities as well as student employment. Fifty-two percent polled in 1984 oppose a longer school day.

3. EVALUATE A CHILD'S CAPACITY TO LEARN. Assess all areas of a child's development, understand a child's learning style, and put together an Individualized Educational Plan (IEP) for each child. (Children receiving special education already benefit from this type of evaluation.) To succeed, this process requires greater teacher training, an interdisciplinary approach, parental input and cooperation, and, of course, funding to provide the appropriate time and expertise.

"Learning is optimal when the time a student spends on learning is the same as the time a student needs." It is known that some students require more time to learn than others; however, students who learn in shorter time periods will not benefit from increased learning time unless their curriculum is enriched.

4. IMPROVE THE QUALITY OF THE CURRICULUM. Clear goals and evaluation procedures should be set to measure progress and to correct students. Increasing instructional time has a greater effect on the quality of education in math, science, and literature, than in reading and language. These latter subjects are more affected by the home environment, according to John I. Goodlad, in his book *A Place Called School.*

5. IMPROVE THE QUALITY OF INSTRUCTION. Quality instruction includes several methods and styles of teaching: group learning experiences, audio-visual aids discussion, immediate corrective feedback, recognition for work completed, diagnostic testing, and guidance.

Passive teaching, such as lecturing, explaining, rote drill and practice, does not have to preclude these more dynamic methods. Regardless of methods, high expectations, praise, and positive reinforcement are most important. Relevant homework should also be given.

6. RAISE ACADEMIC STANDARDS. When teachers and administrators try to accomplish all the educational and noneducational tasks expected of them, they often allow standards to drop. They become less demanding of their students. "Grade inflation," promoting children to the next grade so that they can be with their friends in spite of their academic failure, and the lowering of graduation and course requirements may occur.

Twenty-five percent of the credits earned by general track high school students are in physical education and health education, work experience outside the school, remedial English and mathematics, and personal service and development courses, such as training for adulthood and marriage.

In many schools, the time spent learning how to cook and drive counts as much toward a high school diploma as the time spent studying mathematics, English, chemistry, U.S. history, or biology.

To raise standards, different methods must be used and combined. These include offering less nonacademic course work for credit, instruction by mastery learning techniques, competency testing, and an emphasis on basic academics.

7. CREATE A GOOD SCHOOL ENVIRONMENT. Classrooms should be welcoming. The environment can be enriched by displaying student projects in well-kept, brightly lit, well-ventilated rooms. Classrooms should be places in which students can learn and work under optimum conditions. Teachers, parents, and students are all responsible for ensuring that classroom behavior is conducive to learning.

8. ELIMINATE, AS MUCH AS POSSIBLE, NON-ACADEMIC SCHOOL FUNCTIONS AND COURSES. In general, there is agreement as to which academic courses are essential for students. Math, English, history/government, science, business, foreign language,

and health education courses are considered to be most important for the college-bound student. The same courses, with the exception of foreign language, are seen as important for those not planning to attend college.

There is much debate as to what courses are essential. Many nonacademic courses are added to the curriculum because of what the community perceives as social need. But these courses are not offered to every student. Nor are they necessarily balanced, well researched, or taught in a manner that presents all viewpoints. Nonacademic courses should be selected and evaluated carefully. Explore the advantages of offering nonacademic courses outside the school. Each community, school, and school board should study what nonacademic courses could best be offered in the school and which ones could be sponsored or offered by outside agencies after school hours. Examples of this could be:

Driver Education: sponsored by insurance companies/car dealerships

CPR classes: sponsored by the local fire department/hospital

9. UTILIZE MORE DIVERSE PATHS OF INSTRUCTION. This is a way to improve the quality of education without increasing the number of teachers. Using many different approaches to teach reinforces learning and reaches more students who may learn better if more than one method is used. These methods include:

- Offering computer-based instruction for individualized practice, drills, and exercises.
- Having advanced students work with lower-level students.
- Placing tracked students in heterogeneous groups for a specific time and purpose to enrich their learning experience.
- Encouraging other agencies and groups to assume instruction where appropriate after the "academic day" —for example, drama classes taught by local theater group members, driver education taught by qualified insurance company representatives.

10. USE POSITIVE REINFORCEMENT AT HOME TO

INCREASE A CHILD'S LEARNING CAPACITY. Many educators believe that if a student is given more time to learn, he will take that time to increase his knowledge in a subject. By working with your child at home, you extend the time that your child devotes to that subject. Praising your child for completed work increases your child's desire to continue working and gaining your approval.

PRESCHOOL EDUCATION

One strategy to increase time-on-task is to begin your child's schooling early. *In every task the most important thing is the beginning, and especially when you deal with anything young and tender.*—PLATO. Preschool education is a growing phenomenon in this country. There are movements to incorporate preschools into the established school systems. But formal preschool education may not be for every child. There are differences in family situations and in the developmental levels of children that may delay or defer it. Research indicates that a child's successful educational experiences, whether at home or at preschool, are crucial:

- Before the age of 4, a child develops 50 percent of his intelligence.
- Physiologically, 90 percent of a child's brain is formed by age 5.
- Most intellectual growth occurs before the age of 8. Growth includes the development of learning strategies, learning processes, attitudes, and values.

Though the family is the most significant factor in a child's education during the preschool years, many families are turning to daycare and preschools because of the needs of the increasing number of mothers who are entering the workforce, single parents, and the growing belief in the desirability of preschool experiences. In other countries, the business, government, and religious sectors have taken steps to provide better, earlier, and more affordable daycare and preschools.

In this country, daycare facilities and programs vary widely. In many states private daycare is not regulated by the state except in areas of health, safety, and teacher/child ratio. Usually, states do not require daycare teachers to have any educational training or certification. It is the individual center that sets standards for teachers and the program. Good, affordable daycare should be available to any parent needing that alternative for his child. An example of a program meeting those criteria is the Headstart program. By starting children earlier in education, it affords them more time-on-task.

"Added" time to your child's formal education is significant for future success. But regardless of whether or not you send your child to a preschool, his environment should be enriching. The pre-school ages are critical for later successful learning experiences. These are the years when your child "learns to learn." You must interact with your child, whether or not he attends preschool. It is your responsibility at home to ensure your child's future learning success.

HOW YOU CAN INCREASE THE AMOUNT OF TIME YOUR CHILD SPENDS ON LEARNING

Review again the time-on-task charts for the three elementary schools on the first pages of this chapter. Even the addition of a seemingly short amount of time will help your child learn. For example, consider how much time-on-task a child gains if a parent spends:

- 10 minutes per day x 180 days = 30 hours of extra instruction
- 15 minutes per day x 180 days = 45 hours of extra instruction
- 30 minutes per day x 180 days = 90 hours of extra instruction

Use the following chart to arrange a weekly and monthly schedule for yourself to help your child increase his time-on-task. This schedule can be used to measure the time you help your child at home on his school academics. In each day's box, indicate the number of hours or minutes you plan to help your child and the actual amount of time you spend. Try to equal (or exceed!) your goal.

At home, help your child by interpreting instructions, proofreading work, or checking for neatness. If your child is having difficulty in school, contact his teacher for additional homework to build and reinforce his skills and to provide him with more time-on-task. This extra homework may require your monitoring and interaction. If your child is doing well in school, it is still important for you to take time to work with him. For example, continue to read with him or monitor his homework. Talk to him about his school day. This shared time provides your child with greater incentive to develop and use the skills he has learned at school.

"Helping Your Child" Schedule
(Hours or minutes per day)

WEEK 1

	SUN	MON	TUE	WED	THU	FRI	SAT
GOAL							
ACTUAL							

TOTAL _____

WEEK 2

	SUN	MON	TUE	WED	THU	FRI	SAT
GOAL							
ACTUAL							

TOTAL _____

WEEK 3

	SUN	MON	TUE	WED	THU	FRI	SAT
GOAL							
ACTUAL							

TOTAL _____

WEEK 4

	SUN	MON	TUE	WED	THU	FRI	SAT
GOAL							
ACTUAL							

TOTAL _____

4 weeks total instruction time _____

How much impact can a teacher have on a student, considering all these time factors? ". . . No matter how effective a particular teacher is, each teacher interacts with the child only over a particular school term and is then replaced by a succession of other teachers in later school terms . . ." Parents are with a child throughout the school years. Teachers can give educational skills, but only parents can give the constant psychological and emotional support and additional time needed by their children. Who cannot afford this time for their children?

NINE

THE FUTURE
WITH PARENT POWER

Schools are a living prayer, a mix of all that is great and all that is bad in our society; a coming together that sends sparks of light into the darkest corner of this nation, lending the light of hope to those who will find it in no other institution in America. Everything that America is or hopes to be depends upon what happens in the public school classrooms.

FROSTY TROY

In the last two decades our schools have been given many of the social, medical, ethical, political, and economic problems that society has been unable or unwilling to solve. These problems were once solved in the community, by the family, or by the church. Today's schools are being pushed to become all things to all people. Educators have never asked to be the ones to address these problems, and parents should be extremely concerned that the schools have been given the responsibility for the solutions.

Educators have only five or six hours a day to teach your child correct spoken and written language, reading, and math, as well as the skills needed for other academic subjects. If the majority of school time is spent trying to discipline your child, to teach your child about sex, drugs, AIDS, and traffic safety, and to deal with a hundred other responsibilities that parents should be handling, then there is little time left to teach the academic curriculum for which educators are responsible and for which they should be held accountable.

You as a parent should be asking yourself, "What should I be teaching my child? Do I want the schools to take on more parental responsibilities? Do I want less time spent in the schoolhouse on quality academic courses in order to give the teacher time to handle parental responsibilities?" If you do prefer less time for academics, then don't complain because Johnny can't read or add! You should be saying, "We will not take it anymore. It is unfair for my child to receive an inferior education because other parents are not accepting their parenting responsibilities."

WHY PARENT POWER IS NEEDED TODAY

Certainly the traditional family, with a stay-at-home parent, grandparents nearby, relatives living in the same community for generations, is no longer traditional. The family structure has changed and will continue to change as indicated by these statistics:

- Working mothers: 54.4 percent of all mothers work full time.
- Nineteen percent of today's children live in single-parent households with their mothers. These single-parent families are more likely to have lower incomes.
- One-fourth of all elementary school students are latchkey children.
- There are currently 35 million step families in the United States today.
- The divorce rate in the U.S. is 4.9 per thousand.
- Both parents work in 49.2 percent of all households.
- By 1990 both parents will be working outside of the home in 65 percent of all families.
- More than half the population changes residences every five years.

These factors indicate that parental home-based support is more critical today than ever. Yet some parents use these factors as excuses for not doing their jobs. They call upon the school to assume the role of parent. It is the school that tackles this problem by providing extended daycare, providing medical and nutritional programs, supervising homework, and policing attendance. These measures may be helpful and seen as necessary by a large segment of the parenting community. In spite of these latchkey programs, parents must still be accountable for the traditional tasks and responsibilities of parenting. Nothing negates a parent's responsibilities for his child. A parent shirking the responsibilities of the parenting role affects his child's potential education and all of society.

TODAY'S EDUCATIONAL GOALS

It is your responsibility as a parent to work with educators to set the educational goals for your child. Call for a new agenda for parents which emphasizes a close and supportive relationship with teachers, administrators, and the school to meet mutually articulated educational goals. Teaching these goals as part of the curriculum requires expert programs, excellent teaching, and ongoing support from parents throughout a child's school years. These goals must be emphasized at home as well as in the schoolhouse. As you review the list, note that the goals listed under the first three headings are tasks traditionally given to the schools, while the goals listed under the last two headings are more traditionally assumed by parents. In recent Gallup polls, parents favored educational goals that give students the skills to:

Improve academically
 • Speak and write correctly
 • Understand science and technology
 • Understand and use computers
 • Understand world history and current politics
 • Appreciate the arts
 • Understand U.S. history and the political process
 • Gain more knowledge
 • Promote physical development and health

Continue with one's education
 • Prepare for college

- Develop lifelong learning habits that will enable him to develop new skills in a constantly changing world

Be successfully employed
- Understand the rewards and requirements of different jobs
- Get specialized training for a professional career
- Prepare and plan for post-high school life
- Develop good work habits
- Find good jobs
- Gain financial security
- Have an easier and better life than one's parents did
- Open doors and create opportunities

Achieve personally desirable traits
- Develop the desire to excel
- Critically think things through
- Overcome personal problems
- Develop self-discipline
- Cope with the problems and responsibilities of adulthood
- Achieve self-realization and personal development
- Become independent
- Lead a happy life

Build a value system
- Develop standards of right and wrong
- Develop basic individual values
- Learn respect for law and order
- Get along with others and respect other races, religions, nations, and cultures
- Become better citizens
- Appreciate the "good things in life"
- Contribute to society

The parent action plans presented throughout this book are guidelines which you can follow to achieve these goals. You can and will make a significant difference in your child's success at school even if you do nothing more than let your child know you expect him to get the best education. There are very few geniuses, and your child may not be one, but your job is to make sure he uses his innate abilities to the optimum.

EDUCATIONAL ACHIEVEMENTS

"By any rational standards, Americans should be happy with their schools." Too often, schools are not judged for what they have achieved but by what they are still lacking. American schools have made many positive accomplishments. These should be valued and reinforced, forming the foundation for future success for all our children. Here are some of those accomplishments:

1. "We have made the ideal of mass education work more successfully than any other place on earth." "We have a long record, a century and a half of leading the world in popular education." Diane Ravitch, Professor of Education, Columbia University.

2. Each generation of American-educated students is more schooled than the preceding one.

3. Seventy-five percent of those attending high school graduate. A greater proportion of United States students graduate from high school than is the case in any other country. Contrast this with U.S. graduating students in the year 1900; then, ninety-four percent did not complete high school.

4. More students in the United States have access to higher education and continue their studies in colleges and universities (53 percent) than students in any other country.

5. The teachers in the schools have socialized many immigrant populations into "American norms, values, and beliefs." They have transmitted the dominant culture as a model.

6. The education system was the focal point of the Supreme Court's decision (Brown vs. Board of Education) on integration. As a result, schools initiated busing of children and other desegregation measures. This achievement has not been without problems or critics. But there is no reason why schools should not continue to strive to provide all our children with an equal opportunity to reach their educational potential in an environment that accepts and appreciates differences.

7. In spite of problems within the public education sys-

tem, there has not been a mass exodus to private schooling:

Year	% of students in public schools	% of private school students
Fall 1979	89.9%	10.1%
Fall 1985	89 %	11 %

8. Thanks to our schools, America has one of the highest literacy rates of any society, past and present.
9. Handicapped children formerly kept home or institutionalized are now enrolled in public school programs.
10. Education has contributed to economic productivity. "Two-thirds of the growth in productivity is attributable to the combined effects of applied knowledge, new technology, and educational experiences of the labor force."
11. From 1976 to 1985, forty-seven of the eighty-nine Nobel Prize recipients in the world were Americans.
12. An academic secondary school education is open to all. Other countries track students into academic, vocational, or general high schools. The United States has comprehensive high schools which offer a variety of courses to all students according to their abilities.
13. Secondary schools offer many elective subjects, enabling students to pursue and develop interests in many fields. Critics believe that this is a weakness of the system because electives reduce academic time-on-task. To meet this criticism, schools must offer electives that are academically sound. Schools must advise their students to select the courses that would be most beneficial for them.
14. When a student completes his elementary and secondary schooling he is always eligible to attend a college or university. Even if a student has done poorly, he has the opportunity to earn equivalent degrees or to make up deficiencies by taking college-level remedial course work. These extra chances for success are not common in other countries.
15. In many communities around the country, schools and

school districts are acclaimed for outstanding programs that have been successful in resolving many problems concerning today's youth. These programs cover a broad range including peer pressure counseling, academic recognition assemblies and decathlons, parental workshops, business-school partnerships, drop-out prevention, latchkey programs, etc.

More than any other American institution, the public school system has been shaped by the people in the community it serves. From that community, citizens have elected school board members, sent their children to its elementary and secondary schools, attended school plays and athletic events, and volunteered time to benefit their school. The people helped build the school into a community educational, social, and cultural center. The traditional and most basic aims of the United States school system have been:

- To safeguard freedom and democracy
- To enable the country to produce needed goods and services
- To make the country competitive in the world marketplace
- To maintain and build morality by imparting society's goals and values
- To enable people to rise above circumstances and master the future—to realize the "American dream"
- To produce men and women leaders to guide us
- To give students a basic core of knowledge
- To create a sence of community and purpose in this country—to "Americanize" all citizens by giving them a common core of knowledge

The American public education system has evolved into an open system with access for all. That is its strength. It attempts to do something never tried by any other society—to provide an education for every child. Access to this public education is not limited by a child's religion, ethnic background, sex, language, or handicaps, or by his parents' class, professions, or politics. It is the only such education system in the world with these characteristics. The fact that ours is an open system permits greater opportunity and choice for everyone. Children can acquire the skills they need to succeed. Yet, schools alone cannot give your child all the skills needed to ensure his success.

WHAT SCHOOLS CAN DO WITH YOUR HELP

As a parent, you should ask yourself, "What should I be teaching my child?" Years ago, the basic answer was survival skills. In past American societies, young children learned from observing their parents accomplish essential household chores such as preparing food, building furniture, planting, and sewing. Work was accomplished either in the home or within the town. A parent with a trade may have been followed by a young son who learned that trade by watching and then helping so he, in turn, learned the necessary skills to make his own living. When children did attend schools it was usually just to gain a basic knowledge of the three Rs. Children understood what their parents did for a living and what was necessary to learn to survive.

Today's children have greater opportunities but less understanding of what educational skills are needed to succeed when these opportunities are presented. Thanks to modern conveniences of the industrial age, young children do not often see parents prepare food, build furniture, plant, and sew. Much work today is accomplished in the office, over the phone, or in another community where parents travel by car, train, or airplane. Frequently a young child has a limited understanding of what a parent does at work. Titles such as "Administrative Assistant," "Supervisor," and "Coordinator" do little to add to a child's understanding, especially if that child never sees the parent in the work setting. The occupations portrayed in the media are the ones best understood by children. Yet, the portrayal of even these jobs is often exaggerated for dramatic and comedic plot purposes. Even if a child understands what a parent's job entails, the child may not make the connection between the educational skills required and the opportunity to succeed on the job.

What is it then that parents should be teaching their children? The school curriculum is carefully prescribed by federal mandates, state requirements, the school board, and the school district policy. This curriculum, ranging from academics to the solution of social problems, health care, safety, and many other issues, is constantly growing. Society tells educators what they must teach. Educators then coordinate and articulate the curriculum into what the students must learn. The authors' major effort throughout the *Parent Power* handbook is to provide parents the basic skills so they can assure their child's success in school. Parents should never become so comfortable and satisfied with the school curriculum that they think, "We don't have to teach him THAT, he's learning THAT in school." (That can be anything from sex education, discipline, respect for others, or the work ethic, to managing one's money.)

The parent curriculum is and should be even richer and more complex than the school curriculum. It is the parent who is giving the child the basics of wanting to learn. It is the parent who is stimulating a child's curiosity, sharing values, encouraging questions, praising, correcting, and being a constant role model. Waiting until a child is of school age and then presenting the child at the schoolhouse door with the admonition, "Here, educate him," is a disservice to the teacher, parent, and most of all the child.

Parents, you now have the tools and skills to help your child make the most of the opportunities presented in the American educational system. Our youngsters today are as bright and curious as ever before—perhaps more so. Our children are the best we have. It is up to you to make sure your children get the best education they can. Our society depends upon you. Do not negate your parental responsibilities or allow other parents to do so. What you expect from your child is what you will receive from him. We challenge each of you to:

1. Encourage your child to have faith in his ideas, even if everyone tells him that he is wrong. He should have the conviction to stand up and fight for what he believes is right.
2. Give your child the strength not to follow the crowd when everyone else does. He should be his own greatest critic. He must believe that he is "important and worth whatever effort is necessary to sustain his physical and mental well-being, retain his self-respect, and achieve fulfillment of his potential."
3. Teach your child to filter what he hears through a screen of truth, accepting the information that comes through.
4. Allow your child to choose the career that is "right" for him. His choices should be unlimited and his own. The world needs creativity and talents of all kinds.
5. Encourage your child to sell his ideas and talents to the

highest bidder, but never to put a price tag on his heart and soul.

6. Teach your child not to be afraid of failure. It is better to risk failure than to fail risking. It is far more honorable to fail than to cheat. Teach him not to blame others if he fails in an endeavor.

7. Help your child strive to accept the challenges life places before him and do his best to meet them.

8. Teach your child to do his best—not to aim for mediocrity and be satisfied. Excellence should be his goal in every pursuit. Your child should heed this advice:

   - "You forfeit your chance for life at its fullest when you withhold your best effort . . . When you give only the minimum . . . you receive only the minimum in return. Take hold of your life, apply your gifts and talents, work with dedication and self-discipline. Have high expectations for yourself and convert every challenge into an opportunity."
   - "When you work to your full capacity, you can hope to attain the knowledge and skills that will enable you to create your future and control your destiny. If you do not, you will have your future thrust upon you by others."
   - "Embrace the word 'maximum.' Most people do not live as long as they could, accomplish as much as they are able, or derive as much from life as they might. To do better than this, your mind and body must serve you well for the greatest number of years possible and you can do much toward attaining this end. At all stages of life set goals of both vocation and avocation that call for the best you have to offer."
   - "Getting the most out of life—in essence out of each hour—does not necessarily have anything to do with prestige, money, or power, although all of these have their places in our society. Rather you must decide what is of sufficient concern to you to be worth your maximum effort and whether you pursue it with many, a few, or alone, do so with vigor."

9. Show your child how to keep a sense of humor about himself.

10. Help your child remember to stop and smell the roses.

Life includes more than success measured by fame and fortune.

Society's many problems will never be totally solved, but we must begin with our children. Helping a child succeed in school does not stop when a child enters the school system. It intensifies. Now there is a partnership being formed to help your child. As a parent, you must maximize that partnership so your child can benefit to the utmost of his ability. In order for the schools to continue to meet traditional educational goals and to provide an excellent education system, it is imperative for all parents to supply supportive actions and attitudes. Our country needs to have children who can compete with their counterparts in other parts of the world. Parents must work with educators to make the following recommendations into realities in their schools:

- Give priority to the basics (English, math, reading, and writing).
- Broaden the concept of teaching academic subjects by upgrading "new" basics such as art, music, science, physical education, and civics.
- Increase standards by favoring excellence. Focus on achievement and programs in the academic areas.
- Promote more respect for each other: parents for teachers—teachers for parents. Recognize and encourage the best.
- Lengthen the school day and school year.
- Encourage the assignment of more and meaningful homework.
- Develop an individual educational program specifically designed for each child, monitored by the parents and the school.
- Be aware of current educational issues facing your community and state. Write the media and legislature regarding educational issues that concern you.
- Support the schools with adequate monies.
- Galvanize support for the schools from all segments of the community. Attend school board meetings and urge nonparents to attend.

These recommendations are not impossible to achieve. Indeed, in the best schools, these measures are realities. The driving force in attaining these goals are the parents. Three elements must work together to achieve the "perfect school" environment for students. These are the parents, the administration and staff, and the community at large. The strongest link in this chain is the parents. If active, ongoing parent support is not forthcoming, the best staff and greatest principal cannot compensate, and support from the rest of the community will be lacking.

The victims of this failure to form an educational coalition for excellence are foremost the children, but ultimately, all of society. Only you, as a parent exercising your parent power, can make the big difference for your child.

NOTES

Introduction

1 *"each generation of . . ."* National Commission on Excellence in Education, *An Open Letter to the American People: A Nation at Risk: The Imperative for Educational Reform, A Report to the Nation and the Secretary of Education* (Washington, D.C.: Government Printing Office, April, 1983), p. 11.

2 *"school systems in . . ."* Benjamin Bloom, *All Our Children Learning: A Primer for Parents, Teachers and Other Educators* (New York: McGraw-Hill, 1981), p. 91. Modified from Bloom's work on the Dave study.

3 *"you know you . . .* work and commitment." *A Nation at Risk*, pp. 34–36.

Chapter One
PARENTS, STUDENTS, AND SCHOOLS

5 *"Parents are the . . . their children's educators."* Universal Declaration of Human Rights of the United Nations Charter.

5 *"The effect that . . ."* Neil Postman and Charles Wiengartner, *The School Book* (New York: Dell, 1973), p. 17.

5 *Your child's education . . .* National School Public Relations Association, *A Parent's Guide: Helping Your Child Learn* (Arlington, Virginia: National School Public Relations Association, n.d.), p. 4.

6 *"Through the formative . . ."* Herbert J. Walberg, "Families as Partners in Educational Productivity," *Phi Delta Kappan*, LXV (February 1984), p. 397.

6 *Parent Action: What . . . time or money.* Bloom, p. 101.

8 *A Child's Ten* . . . Adapted from Dr. Kevin Leman, *Parenthood without Hassles—Well, Almost,* Harvest House, 1979.

9 *"Parents suffer if . . ."* Thomas Gordon, *T.E.T.—Teacher Effectiveness Training* (New York: Peter H. Wyden, 1974), pp. 323–324.

10 *Public Lack of* . . . Alec M. Gallup, "The Seventeenth Annual Gallup Poll of the Public's Attitudes toward Public School," *Phi Delta Kappan, LXVII* (September 1985), pp. 42–43.

10 *Teachers/Parent apathy* . . . Alec Gallup, "The Gallup Poll of Teachers' Attitudes toward the Public Schools," *Phi Delta Kappan, LXVI* (October 1984), pp. 104–105.

10 *"If our American educational* . . ." Elsie J. Smith and Clement B. G. London, "Overview: A Union of School, Community and Family," *Urban Education, XVI* (October 1981), p. 249.

10 "Education for the . . ." Sarah Lawrence Lightfoot, "Toward Conflict and Resolution: Relationships between Families and Schools," *Theory into Practice, XX* (Spring 1981), p. 100.

10 *"When teachers and* . . ." M. Donald Thomas, *Parents Have Rights, Too!* ed. Donald W. Robinson, Fastback Series Edition, Vol. CXX (Bloomington: Phi Delta Kappan, 1978), p. 36.

14 *". . . paying for education* . . ." *A Nation at Risk,* pp. 15–16.

14 *"What goes on* . . ." Keith Melville, ed., *Priorities for the Nation's Schools, National Issues Forum* (Dayton: Prepared by the Public Agenda Foundation for the Domestic Policy Agency, 1983), p. 8.

14 *One out of* . . . Harold L. Hodgkinson, "Policy Problems Mandated by Recent Demographic Changes," *Demographic Digest,* n.d., p. 3.

15 *The United States has* . . . Keith Melville, ed., *Priorities for the Nation's Schools,* p. 8.

16 *Considering that the economic* . . . Leroy V. Goodman, ed., *The Education Almanac* 1986-1987 (Alexandria, Virginia: National Association of Elementary School Principals, 1987), p. 24.

16 *One-third of* . . . Paul Copperman, *The Literacy Hoax* (New York: Morrow Quill Paperbacks, 1980), p. 204.

16 *A Gallup Poll* . . . Philip and Susan Jones, *Parents Unite!* (New York: Wyden Books, 1976), p. 31.

Chapter Two
ACADEMICS PLUS

22 *Reading is a* . . . Bruce Baron, Christine Baron and Bonnie MacDonald, *What Did You Learn in School Today?* (New York: Warner Books, 1983), p. 55.

22 *One study of* . . . Donald Lambro, "Practical Ways to Improve Reading Skills in Schools," *Orange County Register,* July 16, 1985, p. A11.

22 *It has been* . . . Sherwood Harris and Lorna B. Harris, *The Teacher's Almanac* 1986-1987 (New York: Facts on File, 1986), p. 240.

24 *"Writing holds us* . . ." Ernest L. Boyer, *High School: A Report on Secondary Education in America* (New York: Harper & Row, 1983), p. 90.

25 *"In our verbal* . . ." Boyer, p. 92.

26 *"Research has shown* . . ." H. Dean Evans, "We Must Begin Educational Reform 'Every Place at Once,'" *Phi Delta Kappan, LXV* (February 1984), p. 176.

26 *Another recent survey* . . . Thomas Lickona, *Raising Good Children* (New York: Bantam Books, 1983), p. 359.

33 *Proficiency in a* . . . *A Nation at Risk,* p. 26.

38 *"Expenditures authorized by* . . ." Alan Weisberg, President of Community Systems Associates, Oakland, CA., "What Research Has to Say about Vocational Education and the High Schools," *Phi Delta Kappan, LXIV* (January 1983), p. 355.

38 *"Meet the needs* . . ." John T. Goodlad, *A Place Called School: Prospects for the Future* (New York: McGraw-Hill, 1984), p. 14.

39 *Keep in school* . . . Weisberg, p. 356.

39 *If your child* . . . Weisberg, p. 357.

40 *Today, big business* . . . "Businesses Supply Learning Opportunities," *USA Today* (January 28, 1985), p. 3D.

40 *Today's kindergartners must* . . . Carol Stevens, "Completely Different Than We Were," *USA Today* (January 2, 1985), p. A1.

40 *They may be* . . . Ibid.

40 *"Asked whether they* . . ." Welford W. Wilms, "Vocational Education and Job Success: The Employer's View," *Phi Delta Kappan, LXIV* (January 1984), p. 349.

41 *Those who find* . . . Weisberg, p. 356.

42 *Today there are* . . . Leslie A. Hait, *Human Brain & Human Learning* (New York: Longman, Inc., 1983), p. 8.

42 *"Even with a* . . ." Stevens, p. A2.

42 *Where will the* . . . Weisberg, p. 357.

42 *The highest paying* . . . Marvin Cetron, Barbara Soriano and Mar-

165

garet Gayle, "Looking Ahead: Jobs and Education in the Future," *The School Administrator* (January 1984), p. 10.

42 *There will be* . . . Ibid.

Chapter Three
AFTER-SCHOOL TIME: HOMEWORK, STUDYING, AND TELEVISION

48 *Forty percent of* . . . Alec M. Gallup, "The Seventeenth Annual Gallup Poll of the Public's Attitudes toward the Public Schools," *Phi Delta Kappan LXVII* (September 1985), p. 42.

48 *According to 47 percent* . . . Ibid., p. 42.

48 *The amount of* . . . Paul Copperman, *The Literacy Hoax* (New York: Morrow Quill Paperbacks, 1980).

48 *Two-thirds of* . . . Keith Melville, ed., *Priorities for the Nation's Schools*, National Issues Forum (Dayton: Prepared by the Public Agenda Foundation for the Domestic Policy Agency, 1983), p. 19.

52 *"The teachings of* . . ." Neil Postman, "Engaging Students in the Great Conversation," *Phi Delta Kappan, LXIV* (January 1983), p. 314.

52 *A Michigan State* . . . Joan Anderson, "Breaking the T.V. Habit."

53 *TV disturbs brain* . . . J. A. Wilkins, "Why Is This Child Always Watching?", *Health, XIII* (August 1981). Reprint Requests for Information, p. 13.

53 *The average two-* . . . Mark S. Hoffman, ed., *World Almanac and Book of Facts 1987* (New York: Pharos Books, 1986), p. 372.

53 *Kindergarten graduates have* . . . Jim Trelease, *Read-Aloud Handbook* (New York: Penguin Books, 1982), p. 23.

53 *Grade school students* . . . Lickona, *Good Children* (New York: Bantam Books, 1983), p. 351.

53 *Students watching no* . . . Office of Educational Research and Improvement, U.S. Dept. of Education. Elementary and Secondary Education Indicators in Brief, 1987. (Washington, D.C.: Superintendent of Documents, 1986), p. 34.

53 *The average cartoon* . . . Lickona, p. 354.

53 *The lexicon of* . . . Michael Lieberman of East Stroudsburg State in *Journal of Reading* (April 1983), in Gerald W. Bracey, "Research: TV Talk Too Terse," *Phi Delta Kappan* (September 1984), p. 69.

53 *By age 12,* . . . Lickona, *Good Children*, p. 353.

53 *Lower achievers* . . . Alice Sterling Honig, "Television and Young Children," *Young Children, XXXVIII* (May 1983), p. 63.

53 *Aggressive children "act up"* . . . Ibid.

53 *By the time* . . . Lickona, *Good Children*, p. 351.

53 *By age 18,* . . . Honig, p. 63.

53 *By the age* . . . Postman, p. 311.

55 *Watching television from* . . . John T. Guthrie, "TV Effects on Achievement," *The Reading Teacher, XXXVI* (March 1983), p. 733.

56 *One study found* . . . J. A. Wilkins, "Why Is This Child Always Watching?" *Health* magazine, *XIII* (August 1981), pp. 39–41, 58–60.

57 *When learning new* . . . Honig, p. 63.

Chapter Four
SPECIAL PROGRAMS

61 *Almost 12 percent* . . . Keith Melville, ed., *Priorities for the Nation's Schools, National Issues Forum* (Dayton: Prepared by the Public Agenda Foundation for the Domestic Policy Agency, 1983), p. 23.

61 *These programs may* . . . Ibid.

61 *Critics of mainstreaming*, Melville, p. 26.

61 *It has been* . . . Ibid.

62 *It is estimated* . . . Melville, ed., p. 23.

63 *In general, 3 to 5 percent* . . . Marsha M. Correll, *Teaching the Gifted and Talented*, ed. Donald W. Robinson, Fastback Series Edition, Vol. CXIX (Bloomington: *Phi Delta Kappan*, 1978), p. 12.

65 *A gifted student* . . . Ibid., p. 8.

65 *"Over half the . . ."* *A Nation at Risk*, p. 8.

66 *These families are* . . . Benjamin S. Bloom, *Developing Talent in Young People* (New York: Ballantine, 1985).

67 *Do not pressure . . . abilities or accomplishments.* Jackie Mallis, *Diamonds in the Dust: Discover and Develop Your Child's Gifts* (Austin, Texas: Multi Media Arts, 1983), pp. 163–165.

68 *". . . in the earliest . . . achieve."* Ernst L. Boyer, *To Save Our Children* (New York: ABC News, Show #1234, 9/4/84), p. 24.

68 *"We have unwisely . . ."* S. I. Hayakawa Ph.D., Honorary Chairman of U.S. English, former U.S. Senator.

69 *Hispanics comprise the* . . . Melville, p. 26.

Chapter Five
MOTIVATING YOUR CHILD TO SUCCEED

71 *"What a person . . ."* Marva Collins, *The Marva Collins Way* (Los Angeles: J. P. Tarcher, Inc., 1982), p. 58.

75 *Two hundred and . . . Take a bow.* Some of these phrases are from Edward B. Fry, Jacqueline K. Polk, and Dona Fountoukidis, *The Reading Teacher's Book of Lists* (Englewood Cliffs, New Jersey: Prentice Hall, 1984). pp. 175–177.

79 Boys are more . . . time explore more. Mallis, p. 134.

79 Girls are more . . . better manual dexterity. Ibid.

79 *Women comprise 51 percent . . .* John W. Wright, *The American Almanac of Jobs and Salaries* (New York: Avon, 1984), p. 745.

79 *. . . earn only $.69 . . .* Wright, *The American Almanac*, p. 651.

79 *. . . $14,479; the median . . .* Bureau of the Census, U.S. Dept. of the Census. *Statistical Abstract of the United States* 1986, 106th ed. (Washington, D.C.: Superintendent of Documents, 1985), p. 456.

79 *Seventy percent of . . .* Wright, *American Almanac*, p. 651.

81 *I help my . . .* Denis Waitley, *Seeds of Greatness: The Ten Best-Kept Secrets of Total Success* (Old Tappan, New Jersey: Fleming H. Revell Company, 1983), p. 140.

83 *People are unreasonable . . .* Steven Barrie and Co., Inc., 7 Vincent Circle, Ivyland, PA 18974.

85 *"School is not . . .* Mario Fantini, *Resources for Improving Education* (Fort Lauderdale: Nova University, 1976), p. 113.

87 *Today, there are . . .* Hana Umlauf Lande, ed., *The Work Almanac & Book of Facts 1985* (New York: Newspaper Enterprise Association, 1984), pp. 356–357.

87 *"The interests of . . ."* David Tavel, *Church-State Issues in Education*, ed., George W. Robinson, Fastback Series Edition, CXXIII (Bloomington, *Phi Delta Kappan*, 1979), p. 45.

87 *The Supreme Court . . .* Nicholas Piediscalzi and William E. Collie, *Teaching about Religion in Public Schools* (Niles, Illinois: Argus Communications, 1977), p. 15.

88 *". . . make moral education . . ."* Ralph L. Mosher, "Parenting for Moral Growth," *Journal of Education*, CLXII (Summer 1981), p. 244.

92 *"You must come . . ."* Marva Collins, p. 22.

Chapter Six
SETTING LIMITS: WAYS TO IMPROVE
YOUR CHILD'S BEHAVIOR

95   *". . . everybody supervised everybody's . . ."* Lickona, *Good Children,* p. 4.

95   *Ninety-four percent . . . child behavior problems.* Alex Gallup, "The Gallup Poll of Teachers' Attitudes toward the Public Schools," *Phi Delta Kappan, LXVI* (October 1984), p. 106.

97   *Whatever strategy is . . .* Spencer Johnson, *The One Minute Father* (New York: William Morrow and Company, 1983), p. 24.

99   *A Parent's Prayer . . .* Garry C. Myers, *Highlights for Children* (quoted from a column by Abigail Van Buren).

107 *"Marble Mania."* Lee Canter and Marlene Canter, *Assertive Discipline for Parents* (New York: Harper & Row, 1982), p. 97.

108 *Children Learn What . . .* Nolte.

109 *". . . give kids enough . . . control they need."* Lickona, *Good Children,* p. 191.

111 *By age fifteen . . .* Bureau of the Census, U.S. Department of the Census. *Statistical Abstract of the United States 1986,* 106th ed. (Washington, D.C.: Superintendent of Documents, 1985), p. 64.

111 *At least 2.5 million . . .* Lickona, *Good Children,* p. 367.

111 *By age twenty . . .* "Teen Pregnancy: Data Implore U.S. to Make Birth Control More Available," *Arizona Daily Star,* 4/23/85, Section A, p. 12.

111 *Teenaged mothers . . .* Bureau of the Census, U.S. Dept. of the Census. *Statistical Abstract of the United States* 1986, 106th ed. (Washington, D.C.: Superintendent of Documents, 1985), p. 62.

111 *By age nineteen . . .* Ibid., p. 66.

112 *The Guttmacher Institute . . .* "Teen Pregnancy: . . ." *Arizona Daily Star,* p. 12.

112 *Seventy-five percent . . .* Alec M. Gallup, "The 17th Annual Gallup Poll of the Public's Attitudes toward the Public Schools," *Phi Delta Kappan, LXVII* (September 1985), p. 40.

113 *The family will . . .* Asta M. Kenney and Margaret Terry Orr, "Sex Education: An Overview of Current Programs, Policies and Research," *Phi Delta Kappan, LXV* (March 1984), p. 494.

115 *A Memorandum from Your Child.* Adapted from Dr. Kevin Leman,

Parenthood without Hassles—Well, Almost, Harvest House, 1979, as quoted in a column by Abigail Van Buren.

Chapter Seven
THE TROUBLED STUDENT

120 *"The school has . . ."* Ernest L. Boyer, *High School: A Report on Secondary Education in America* (New York: Harper & Row, 1983), p. 245.

120 *In 1982 there . . .* U.S. Census Bureau, 1982.

121 *"Mr. Epton was asked . . ."* Mike Royko, "The Reason for School Drop-Outs," *The Chicago Tribune,* 1984.

123 *Many children are . . .* Theodor R. Sizer, "Studies of Schooling: High School Reform—The Need for Engineering," *Phi Delta Kappan, LXIV* (June 1983), p. 681.

124 *"that as many . . ."* Benjamin Bloom, *All Our Children Learning: A Primer for Parents, Teachers and Other Educators* (New York: McGraw-Hill, 1982), p. 18.

125 *repeated failure . . .* Bloom, p. 19.

126 *"Many students find . . ."* Sizer, *Studies of Schooling . . . ,* pp. 680–681.

127 *One-third of . . .* Lickona, *Good Children,* p. 397.

127 *Four out of . . .* David Toma with Irv Levey, *Toma Tells It Straight with Love* (New York: Books in Focus, 1981), p. 119.

127 *Five percent of . . .* Adele Crowe, "Teen Cocaine Use Triples Since 1975," *USA Today,* March 21, 1985, p. A1.

127 *Eighty-five percent . . .* experiment with drugs. Toma, *Toma Tells,* p. 71.

127 *A recent National . . .* "To Save Our Schools, To Save Our Children," *ABC News,* Transcript of Show #1234 (New York: ABC News, 9/4/84), p. 10.

127 *Six percent of . . .* Crowe, *"Teen Cocaine Use . . . ,"* p. A1.

127 *Five percent of . . .* Ibid.

127 *"The importation and . . ."* H. Dean Evans, "We Must Begin Educational Reform 'Every Place at Once,'" *Phi Delta Kappan, LXV* (November 1983), p. 175.

133 *Children who are . . .* Pamela Cantor, "These Teenagers Feel They Have No Options," *People Magazine,* February 18, 1985, p. 84.

134 *Ten Suicide Warnings . . .* Cantor, *". . . No Options,"* p. 87.

Chapter Eight
THE TIME IT TAKES TO LEARN:
UNDERSTANDING THE SCHOOL DAY

135 *Time-on-task* . . . Arizona state law requires 175 days.

135 *Professional educators who* . . . Mario Fantini, *Resources for Improving Education* (Ft. Lauderdale, Florida: Nova University, 1976), p. 98.

136 *The loss of* . . . Manuel J. Justiz, "It's Time to Make Every Minute Count," *Phi Delta Kappan, LXV* (March 1984), p. 483.

136 ". . . *the school year* . . ." Janet H. Caldwell, William G. Huitt, and Anna O. Graeber, "Time Spent in Learning Implications from Research," *Elementary School Journal, LXXXII* (May 1982), pp. 472–473.

136 *The following chart* . . . Ibid., pp. 476–477.

137 *The problem of* . . . Ernest L. Boyer, *High School: A Report on Secondary Education in America* (New York: Harper & Row, 1983), p. 154.

138 *"Two hundred years* . . ." Michael J. Bakalis, "Power and Purpose in American Education," *Phi Delta Kappan, LXV* (September 1983), p. 9.

138 *"Various forces in society* . . ." John I. Goodlad, *What Schools Are For* (Bloomington: *Phi Delta Kappan,* 1979), p. 10.

139 *As educational tasks* . . . Barton R. Clark, "The High School and the University: What Went Wrong in America, Part I," *Phi Delta Kappan, LXVI,* February 1985, p. 393.

140 *These are big* . . . (In Arizona 51 percent of the 506,000 students attending school daily participate in school nutrition programs.) "Advertising Proposal for Arizona's School Food Service Programs."

142 *According to a* . . . George H. Gallup, "The Sixteenth Annual Gallup Poll of the Public's Attitudes toward Public Schools," *Phi Delta Kappan, LXVI* (September 1984), p. 32.

143 *A longer school* . . . American Association of School Administrators handbook, p. 13.

143 *Yet, a longer* . . . George H. Gallup, "Sixteenth Gallup Poll," p. 29.

144 *Fifty-two percent* . . . Ibid.

144 *"Learning is optimal . . ."* Caldwell, Huitt, and Graeber, "Time Spent in Learning," p. 472.

144 *Clear goals and* . . . McGraw-Hill, 1984. John I. Goodlad, *A Place Called School* (New York: McGraw-Hill, 1984), p. 96.

145 *Twenty-five percent . . . A Nation at Risk,* p. 19.

145 *In many schools . . .* National Commission on Excellence in Education, p. 22.

145 *In general there . . .* George H. Gallup, "Sixteenth Gallup Poll," p. 30.

147 *Before the age . . .* Jackie Mallis, *Diamonds in the Dust: Discover and Develop Your Child's Gifts* (Austin, Texas: Multi Media Arts, 1983), p. 4.

147 *Physiologically, 90 percent . . .* John R. Cryan and Elaine Surbek, *Early Childhood Education: Foundations for Lifelong Learning,* ed. Donald W. Robinson, Fastback Series Edition, CXXXIII (Bloomington: *Phi Delta Kappan,* 1979), p. 7.

147 *Most intellectual growth . . .* Ibid.

150 *". . . No matter how . . ."* Benjamin Bloom, *All Our Children Learning: A Primer for Parents, Teachers and Other Educators* (New York: McGraw-Hill, 1981), pp. 90–91.

Chapter Nine
THE FUTURE WITH PARENT POWER

151 *"Schools are a . . ."* Frosty Troy, *Oklahoma Observer,* 11/82.

152 *Working mothers: 54.4 percent . . .* Bureau of the Census. U.S. Department of the Census. *Statistical Abstract of the United States 1986,* 106th ed. Washington, D.C.: Superintendent of Documents, 1985, p. 132.

152 *Nineteen percent of . . .* Ibid., p. 45.

152 *One-fourth of . . .* Alec M. Gallup, "The Seventeenth Annual Gallup Poll of the Public's Attitudes toward Public Schools," *Phi Delta Kappan, LXVII* (September 1985), p. 42.

152 *There are currently . . .* Karen S. Peterson, "It takes work to turn 'yours and mine' into ours,'" p. 5D, *USA Today,* October 29, 1987.

152 *The divorce rate . . .* Bureau of the Census. U.S. Department of the Census. *Statistical Abstract of the United States 1986,* 106th ed. (Washington, D.C.: Superintendent of Documents, 1985), p. 56.

152 *Both parents work . . .* Ibid. p. 399.

152 *By 1990 both . . .* Carol Stevens, "Completely Differently Than We Were," *USA Today,* January 2, 1985, p. A2.

152 *More than half . . .* "Mobility of the Resident Population by State, 1980," *Statistical Abstract of the United States* (Washington, D.C.: U.S. Department of Commerce, Bureau of the Census, 1984), p. 16.

155 *"By any rational . . ."* Paul Goodman, "The Universal Trap," *The Limits of Schooling,* eds. Peter Marin, Vincent Stanley, and Kathryn Marin (Englewood Cliffs, New Jersey: Prentice-Hall, 1975), p. 60.

155 *"We have made . . ."* Michael J. Bakalis, "Power and Purpose in American Education," *Phi Delta Kappan, LXV* (September 1983), p. 8.

155 *"We have a long record."* To Save Our Schools, To Save Our Children, Transcript (New York: 9/4/84 ABC News), p. 27.

155 *Seventy-five percent . . .* Ernest L. Boyer, *High School: A Report on Secondary Education in America* (New York: Harper & Row, 1983), p. 21.

155 *A greater proportion . . .* Paul Goodman, "The Universal Trap," The Limits of Schooling, eds. Peter Marin, Vincent Stanley, and Kathryn Marin (Englewood Cliffs, New Jersey: Prentice-Hall, 1975), p. 60.

155 *More students in . . .* Frosty Troy, *Oklahoma Observer,* November 1982.

155 *The teachers in . . .* John I. Goodlad, *A Place Called School* (New York: McGraw-Hill Book Company, 1984), p. 11.

156 *Fall 1979 89.9% . . .* Office of Educational Research and Improvement, U.S. Dept. of Education. Elementary and Secondary Education Indicators in Brief, 1987 (Washington, D.C.: Superintendent of Documents, 1986), p. 13.

156 *"Two-thirds of . . ."* Richard A. Hersh, "How to Avoid Becoming a Nation of Technopeasants," *Phi Delta Kappan, LXIV* (May 1983), pp. 636–637.

156 *From 1976 to . . .* Mark S. Hoffman, ed. *World Almanac and Book of Facts,* 1987 (New York: Pharos Books, 1986), pp. 350–352.

159 *". . . important and worth . . ."* A Nation at Risk, p. 35.

160 *"You forfeit your . . ."* A Nation at Risk, p. 35.

160 *"When you work . . ."* Everett S. Allen, "See Yourself in a Good, Clean Mirror," *Arizona Daily Star,* June 23, 1985, p. 2E.

160 *"Embrace the word . . ."* A Nation at Risk, p. 35.

160 *"Getting the most . . ."* Ibid.

BIBLIOGRAPHY

BOOKS

Albert, Linda. *Coping with Kids and School.* New York: E. P. Dutton, Inc., 1984.

American Association of School Administrators. *Building Public Confidence in Our Schools.* Arlington, Virginia: American Association of School Administrators, 1983.

American Association of School Administrators. *Time on Task.* Arlington, Virginia: American Association of School Administrators, 1982.

Armstrong, William H. *87 Ways to Help Your Child in School.* Barron's Educational Series. Woodbury, New York: Barron's, 1961.

Baron, Bruce, Christine Baron, and Bonnie MacDonald. *What Did You Learn in School Today?* New York: Warner Books, 1983.

Beauchamp, Edward R. *Education in Contemporary Japan.* ed. Donald W. Robinson. Fastback Series Edition, No. 171. Bloomington: Phi Delta Kappan, 1982.

Beckham, Joseph. *Legal Implications of Minimum Competency Testing,* ed. Donald W. Robinson. Fastback Series Edition, No. 138. Bloomington: Phi Delta Kappan, 1980.

Bell, Terrel H. *Active Parent Concern.* Englewood Cliffs, New Jersey: Prentice-Hall, 1976.

Berger, Eugenia H. *Beyond the Classroom.* St. Louis: Mosby Company, 1983.

Bloom, Benjamin S. *All Our Children Learning: A Primer for Parents, Teachers and Other Educators.* New York: McGraw-Hill, 1981.

Bloom, Benjamin S. *Developing Talent in Young People.* New York: Ballantine, 1985.

Boyer, Ernest L. *High School: A Report on Secondary Education in America.* New York: Harper & Row, 1983.

Brodinsky, Ben. *How a School Board Operates,* ed. Donald W. Robinson. Fastback Series Edition, No. 88. Bloomington: Phi Delta Kappan, 1977.

Canter, Lee, and Marlene Canter. *Assertive Discipline for Parents.* New York: Harper & Row, 1982.

College Board. *Academic Preparation for College: What Students Need to Know and Be Able to Do.* New York: College Entrance Examination Board, 1983.

Collins, Marva. *Marva Collins Way.* Los Angeles: J. P. Tarcher, Inc., 1982.

Collins, Myrtle T. and Dwane R. Collins. *Survival Kit for Teachers (and Parents).* Santa Monica: Goodyear Publishing Company, 1975.

Commager, Henry Steele. *The People and Their Schools,* ed. Donald W. Robinson. Fastback Series Edition, No. 79. Bloomington: Phi Delta Kappan, 1976.

Copperman, Paul. *The Literacy Hoax.* New York: Morrow Quill Paperbacks, 1980.

Correll, Marsha M. *Teaching the Gifted and Talented,* ed. Donald W. Robinson. Fastback Series Edition, No. 119. Bloomington: Phi Delta Kappan, 1978.

Cryan, John R. and Elaine Surbek. *Early Childhood Education: Foundations for Lifelong Learning,* ed. Donald W. Robinson. Fastback Series Edition, No. 133. Bloomington: Phi Delta Kappan, 1979.

DeBruyn, Robert L. and Jack L. Larson. *You Can Handle Them All.* Manhattan, Kansas: The Master Teacher, 1984.

Devine, Thomas G. *Teaching Study Skills.* Boston: Allyn and Bacon, Inc., 1981.

Dodson, Fitzhugh. *How to Discipline with Love.* New York: New American Library, 1978.

Fantini, Mario. *Resources for Improving Education.* Fort Lauderdale, Florida: Nova University, 1976.

Flesch, Rudolf. *Why Johnny Still Can't Read.* New York: Harper & Row, 1981.

Fry, Edward B., Jacqueline K. Polk, and Dona Fountoukidis. *The Reading Teacher's Book of Lists.* Englewood Cliffs, New Jersey: Prentice-Hall, 1984.

Glasser, William. *Schools without Failure.* New York: Harper & Row, 1969.

Goodlad, John I. *A Place Called School: Prospects for the Future.* New York: McGraw-Hill, 1984.

Goodlad, John I. *What Schools Are For.* Bloomington, Indiana: Phi Delta Kappan Educational Foundation, 1979.

Gordon, Thomas. *T. E. T.—Teacher Effectiveness Training.* New York: Peter H. Wyden, 1974.

Hait, Leslie A. *Human Brain and Human Learning.* New York: Longman, Inc., 1983.

Johnson, Spencer. *The One Minute Father.* New York: William Morrow and Company, Inc., 1983.

Jones, Philip and Susan. *Parents Unite!* New York: Wyden Books, 1976.

Kahn, Herman. *The Coming Boom.* New York: Simon & Schuster, 1982.

175

Kappelman, Murray and Paul Ackerman. *Between Parent and School.* New York: The Dial Press, 1977.

Karlin, Muriel Schoenbrun. *Make Your Child a Success: Career Guidance from Kindergarten to College.* New York: Putnam Books, 1983.

Lane, Hana Umlauf, ed. *The World Almanac and Book of Facts, 1985.* New York: Newspaper Enterprise Association, Inc., 1984.

Lickona, Thomas. *Raising Good Children.* New York: Bantam Books, 1983.

Lingens, Hans G. and Barbara Lingens. *Education in West Germany: A Quest for Excellence,* ed. Donald W. Robinson. Fastback Series Edition, No. 140. Bloomington: Phi Delta Kappan, 1980.

Long, Delbert and Roberta Long. *Education in the U.S.S.R.,* ed. Donald W. Robinson. Fastback Series Edition, No. 148. Bloomington: Phi Delta Kappan, 1980.

Maillis, Jackie. *Diamonds in the Dust: Discover and Develop Your Child's Gifts.* Austin, Texas: Multi Media Arts, 1983.

Marin, Peter, Vincent Stanley, and Kathy Marin. *The Limits of Schooling.* Englewood Cliffs, New Jersey: Prentice-Hall, 1975.

Melville, Keith, ed. *Priorities for the Nation's Schools.* National Issues Forum. Dayton, Ohio: Prepared by the Public Agenda Foundation for the Domestic Policy Association.

Nason, Leslie J. *Help Your Child Succeed in School.* New York: Cornerstone Library, 1964.

National Center for Educational Statistics. *The Condition of Education.* Washington D.C.: U.S. Department of Education, 1983.

National Center for Educational Statistics. *Digest of Educational Statistics, 1982.* Washington, D.C.: U.S. Department of Education, 1982.

National Center for Educational Statistics. *Projections of Educational Statistics to 1990-91.* Vol I. Washington, D.C.: U.S. Department of Education, 1982.

National Commission on Excellence in Education. *An Open Letter to the American People: A Nation at Risk: The Imperative for Educational Reform, A Report to the Nation and the Secretary of Education.* Washington, D.C.: Government Printing Office, April 1983.

National School Public Relations Association. *A Parent's Guide to Helping Your Children Learn.* Arlington, Virginia: National School Public Relations Association, n.d.

Piediscalzi, Nicholas and William E. Collie. *Teaching about Religion in Public Schools.* Niles, Illinois: Argus Communications, 1977.

Postman, Neil and Charles Wiengartner. *The School Book.* New York: Dell, 1973.

Ravitch, Diane. *The Schools We Deserve: Reflections of the Educational Crisis of Our Time.* New York: Basic Books, Inc., 1985.

Rioux, William. *You Can Improve Your Child's School.* New York: Simon & Schuster, 1980.

Rosner, Joseph. *Myths of Child Rearing.* New York: Dembner Books, 1983.

Siberman, Charles E. *The Open Classroom.* New York: Random House, 1973.

Tavel, David. *Church-State Issues of Education,* ed. Donald Robinson. Fastback Series Edition, No. 123. Bloomington: Phi Delta Kappan, 1979.

Thomas, M. Donald. *Parents Have Rights Too!,* ed. Donald W. Robinson. Fastback Series Edition, No. 120. Bloomington: Phi Delta Kappan, 1978.

Toma, David with Irv Levey. *Toma Tells It Straight with Love.* New York: Books in Focus, 1981.

Trelease, Jim. *Read-Aloud Handbook.* New York: Penguin Books, 1982.

Waitley, Denis. *Seeds of Greatness: The Ten Best-Kept Secrets of Total Success.* Old Tappan, New Jersey: Fleming H. Revell Company, 1983.

Wright, John W. *The American Almanac of Jobs and Salaries.* New York: Avon Books, 1984.

PERIODICALS

"Advertising Proposal for Arizona's School Food Service Programs," *School Food Service Director,* II (January 2, 1985), 1-3.

Allen, Everett S. "See Yourself in a Good, Clean Mirror," *The Arizona Daily Star,* June 23, 1985.

Bakalis, Michael J. "Power and Purpose in American Education," *Phi Delta Kappan,* LXV (September 1983), 7-13.

Bell, Derrick. "Learning from Our Losses. Is School Desegregation Still Feasible in the 1980's?" *Phi Delta Kappan,* LXIV (April, 1983), 572-575.

Bracey, Gerald W. "Research: TV Talk Too Terse," *Phi Delta Kappan,* LXVI (September, 1984), 69-70.

Bruce, Michael G. "Many Ways to Slice a Common Cake," *Phi Delta Kappan,* LXIV (January, 1983), 370-371.

"Business Supply Learning Opportunities," *USA Today,* January 28, 1985.

Cantor, Pamela. "These Teenagers Feel They Have No Options," *People Magazine,* XXIII (February 18, 1985), 84-87.

Caldwell, Janet, William G. Huitt, and Anna O. Graeber. "Time Spent in Learning: Implications from Research," *Elementary School Journal,* LXXXII (May, 1982), 471-480.

Cetron, Marvine, Barbara Soriano, and Margaret Gayle. "Looking Ahead: Jobs and Education in the Future," *The School Administrator* (January, 1984), 10-12.

Clark, Barton R. "The High School and the University: What Went Wrong in America, Part I," *Phi Delta Kappan,* LXVI (February, 1985), 391-397.

Cogan, John J. "Should the U.S. Mimic Japanese Education? Let's Look Before We Leap," *Phi Delta Kappan,* LXVI (February, 1985), 463-468.

Crowe, Adele. "Teen Cocaine Use Triples Since 1975," *USA Today* (March 21, 1985).

Evans, H. Dean. "We Must Begin Educational Reform 'Every Place at Once,'" *Phi Delta Kappan*, LXV (February 1984), 171-173.

Gallup, Alec. "The Gallup Poll of Teachers' Attitudes toward Public Schools," *Phi Delta Kappan*, LXV (March 1984), 97-107.

Gallup, Alec M. "The Seventeenth Annual Gallup Poll of the Public's Attitudes toward Public Schools," *Phi Delta Kappan*, LXVI (September, 1984), 23-38.

Gallup, George H. "The Sixteenth Annual Gallup Poll of the Public's Attitude toward Public Schools," *Phi Delta Kappan*, LXVII (September, 1985), 35-47.

Guthrie, John T. "TV Effects on Achievement," *The Reading Teacher*, XXXVI (March, 1983), 732-734.

Hersh, Richard A. "How to Avoid Becoming a Nation of Technocrats," *Phi Delta Kappan*, LXIV (May, 1983), 635-638.

Hodgkinson, Harold. "Policy Problems Mandated by Recent Demographic Changes," *Demographic Digest*, n.d.

Honig, Alice Sterling. "Television and Young Children," *Young Children*, XXXVIII (May, 1983), 63-76.

Johnson, Bonnie, ed. "Teen Suicide," *People Magazine*, XXIII (February 18, 1985), 76.

Justiz, Manuel J. "It's Time to Make Every Minute Count," *Phi Delta Kappan*, LXIV (March, 1984), 483-485.

Kenney, Asta M. and Margaret Terry Orr. "Sex Education: An Overview of Current Programs, Policies and Research," *Phi Delta Kappan*, LXV (March, 1984), 491-496.

Lambro, Donald. "Practical Ways to Improve Reading Skills in School," *Orange County Register*, July 16, 1985.

Lightfoot, Sarah Lawrence. "Toward Conflict and Resolution: Relationships between Families and Schools." *Theory into Practice*, XX (Spring, 1981), 97-104.

Marcuccio, Phyllis. "Responding to the Economic Sputnik," *Phi Delta Kappan*, LXV (May, 1983), 618-620.

Mosher, Ralph. "Parenting for Moral Growth," *Journal of Education*, CLXII (Summer, 1981), 244-261.

"National Task Force on Education for Economic Growth," *US News and World Report*, May 16, 1983.

Ovando, Carlos. "Bilingual/Bicultural Education: Its Legacy and Its Future," *Phi Delta Kappan*, LXIV (April, 1983), 564-568.

Postman, Neil. "Engaging Students in the Great Conversation," *Phi Delta Kappan*, LXIV (January, 1983), 310-316.

Royko, Mike. "The Reason for School Drop-Outs," *The Chicago Tribune*, 1984.

Shimara, Nobuo K. "Japanese Education and Its Implications for U.S. Education," *Phi Delta Kappan*, LXVI (February, 1985), 418-421.

Sigda, Robert. "The Crisis in Science Education and the Realities of

Teaching Science in the Classroom," *Phi Delta Kappan,* LXIV (May, 1983), 624-627.

Sizer, Theodore. "Studies of Schooling: High School Reform—The Need for Engineering," *Phi Delta Kappan,* LXIV (June, 1983), 679-683.

Smith, Elsie and Clement B. G. London. "Overview: A Union of School, Community and Family," *Urban Education,* XVI (October, 1981), 247-260.

Stevens, Carol. "Completely Different Than We Are Today," *USA Today,* January 2, 1985.

"Teen Pregnancy: Data Implore U.S. to Make Birth Control More Available," *Arizona Daily Star,* April 23, 1985.

Walberg, Herbert J. "Families as Partners in Educational Productivity," *Phi Delta Kappan,* LXV (February, 1984), 397-400.

Weisberg, Alan. "What Research Has to Say about Vocational Education and the High Schools," *Phi Delta Kappan,* LXIV (January, 1983), 355-359.

Wellborn, Stanley N., Joanne Davidson, Mary Galligan, and Carey W. English. "Signs of Hope for Our Schools," *US News and World Report,* September 7, 1981.

Wilkins, J. A. "Why Is This Child Always Watching?," *Health,* XIII (August, 1981), 39-41, 58-60.

Wilms, Wilford W. "Vocational Education and Job Success: The Employer's View," *Phi Delta Kappan,* LXIV (January, 1984), 347-350.

Wright, Guy. "U.S. English," *San Francisco Sunday Examiner & Chronicle,* n.d.

OTHER SOURCES

ABC News. "To Save Our Schools, To Save Our Children," Transcript from ABC News, New York, September 4, 1984.

"A Child's Ten Commandments to Parents," adapted from *Parenthood without Hassles—Well, Almost* by Kevin Leman.

Huntley, Chet. Address to the National School Boards Association, Anaheim, April, 1973.

"Kids Talk about Discipline: A Memorandum from Your Child," Adapted from the *King's Business Magazine* by the Bible Institute of Los Angeles, Inc., by *International Study Group Newsletter* published by Chicago Council, Community Child Guidance Centers, Inc., November 1963, reproduced from *Leader's Manual for Children: The Challenge* by Draikurs and Soltz, 1967.

Universal Declaration of Human Rights of the United Nations Charter.

Warner, Carolyn. Statement by Arizona State School Superintendent concerning the U.S. Department of Education Deputy's Second State Educational Statistics Report, December 18, 1984.

"What's Right with Our Public Schools?" (reprint from Michigan Association of Secondary School Principals, March, 1982) *Arizona Administrator,* Fall, 1982, p. 9.

INDEX

ability grouping, 59–61
Acquired Immune Deficiency
Syndrome (AIDS), 111, 112,
140, 152
after-school activities, 20, 47–57,
140–142, 146
alcohol, *see* substance abuse
ambition, 44–46
college-bound students and, 45–
46
motivation and, 80–83, 92–93
non-college students and, 44–45
success and, 92–93
arts, 34–35, 161
athletic events, 12, 35–37, 138, 142

Becoming a Nation of Readers, 22
bilingual education, 27, 68–69, 141
Bloom, Benjamin S., 66, 124
Boyer, Ernest L., 120
breakfast, 9, 140
Brown vs. Board of Education, 155
Buckley Amendment, 19

cardio-pulmonary resuscitation
(CPR), 140, 146
career guidance, 41–43, 44
"Children Learn What They Live"
(Nolte), 108
civics, 161
Civil Rights Act (1964), 68

clubs, 142
college
degrees granted by, 41
eligibility for, 156
preparation for, 45–46, 146, 153
statistics on attendance at, 155
Collins, Marva, 92
communities, 1–2
active observers in, 13–14
educational responsibilities of,
146, 162
nonparticipants in, 13
policymakers in, 15, 157
school professionals in, 17
volunteer work in, 14–15, 141–
142
competition, 84–85
computers, 18, 30–31, 146
conferences, 11, 13
contracts, 105
co-op programs, 38, 142
counseling, 130, 157
curriculum, 144
basic courses in, 21–44, 145–146,
161
definition of, 23
laws pertaining to, 37, 63, 68, 158
nonacademic areas in, 136, 138–
142, 145–146
recent changes in, 136
social problems addressed in,
138–142, 151

day care, 140, 143, 147–148
Developing Talent in Young People
    (Bloom), 66
discipline, 95–107, 159
    fifteen strategies for, 99–107
    goal setting and, 3, 105
    lack of, 10
driver education, 140, 146
dropouts, 120–127
drugs *see* substance abuse
dyslexia, 61

education
    bilingual, 27, 68–69, 141
    goals of, 153–154
    laws pertaining to, 17, 19–20, 61
    positive attitudes toward, 5–6, 71
    public perception of, 70, 151
    shared responsibility of, 10, 13–
        14
elementary schools, 48, 53, 136–137
employment
    after-school, 43
    preparation for, 38–45, 154
    realistic expectations of, 40–43
    traditional vs. modern, 158
English as a Second Language
    (ESL), 69, 141
Epton, Bernard, 121

failure, 120–127
    risking of, 8, 160
Family Educational Rights and
    Privacy Act (1974), 19
field trips, 140
foreign languages, 33–34, 145
Freedom of Information Act, 19

Gallup Polls, 9–10, 16, 142, 153
gifted children, 63–68
    parental guidance of, 66–68
    school programs and strategies
        for, 65
    special problems of, 65
goal setting, 9, 81, 83–84
    discipline and, 3, 105
    nine steps to, 84
Goodlad, John I., 144

grade inflation, 145
grooming, 9, 82
Guttmacher Institute, 112

Handicapped Children's Act, 61
handicapped students, 17, 61, 156
Headstart program, 148
health
    parental obligations for, 6, 7–8,
        11
    school programs related to, 35–
        36, 112–113, 139–140, 146
high schools, 53
    statistics on graduation from, 155
hobbies, 7, 30
home economics, 37–38
home environment, 2, 7, 48, 72–74,
    118, 131
homework, 12, 47–50, 118
    parental monitoring of, 11, 48–
        50, 148–149
household chores, 6, 38, 102–103,
    158

illiteracy, 22
illness, 9, 141
Individualized Educational Plan
    (IEP), 61, 144, 161
industrial arts, 37–38
Intelligence Quotient (IQ) tests, 63

job/career fairs, 14
junior high schools, 53
juvenile deliquency, 39, 98

Koop, C. Everett, 112

language development, 3, 6, 7
    speaking and listening skills in,
        25–27, 73–74
    see also bilingual education;
        foreign languages
latchkey programs, 140, 143, 153,
    157
learning agendas, 12–13
learning disabilities, 62–63
Leman, Kevin, 116

libraries, 7, 23
Life, 43
Love, Ruth, 121
lunch/breakfast programs, 140

manners, 114–115
mastery learning, 124–125
mathematics, 3, 18, 27–29, 145, 161
money management, 28, 29, 159
motivation, 70–95
    ambition and, 80–83, 92–93
    goal setting and, 9, 81, 83–84
    independence and, 13, 80, 109
    parental guidance and, 70–71,
        81–83
    pleasure in learning as, 6, 71

*Nation at Risk, A: The Imperative for
    Educational Reform*, 2, 3, 4,
    65–66
National Commission on Excellence
    in Education, 2
National Institute on Drug Abuse,
    127
Nolte, Dorothy Law, 108
nutrition, 9, 11, 30, 37, 38, 140

open houses, 11–12, 18
O'Reilly, Jane, 79
outreach programs, 14

parent-child relationship
    academic aspirations and, 9, 70–
      71
    academic guidance and support
      in, 6–7, 11–12, 18, 21, 22–25,
      28–34, 45–46, 48–52, 123–126,
      146–147, 159–162
    choices offered in, 82
    communication in, 4–5, 7, 8, 23,
      26–27, 57, 73–74, 82, 97, 103–
      104, 119
    guidelines in, 8–9, 115–116
    rewards in, 12, 23, 106, 123
    sensitivity in, 8
*Parenthood Without Hassles—Well,
    Almost* (Leman), 116

parents
    active participation of, 3, 11–13,
      15
    attendance of school events by,
      11–12, 18, 36
    divorce rates of, 152
    ideal qualities in, 99
    personal learning commitment
      of, 3
    responsibilities of, 1, 3, 7–8, 11,
      153, 159–162
    rights of, 3, 5, 17–18
    role modeling by, 3, 8, 86, 114–
      115, 158
    school problems perceived by, 9–
      10
    as task persons, 11, 15
    working mothers as, 152
Parent Teacher Association (PTA),
    15, 138
Parent Teacher Organization (PTO),
    15
parent-teacher relationship, 153
    communication and, 9–10, 11–
      12, 13, 18, 19
    mutual support in, 11, 12
    troubled students and, 119–120
peers
    pressure of, 106–110, 131, 157
    relationships with, 6, 71, 130–131
physical education, 35–37, 145, 161
Place Called School, A (Goodlad),
    144
Plato, 147
Postman, Neil, 5
praise, 23, 71, 72, 74, 75–78, 106,
    125, 147
pregnancy, teenage, 39, 111, 112
preschool education, 147–148
private schools
    boards of, 16–17
    gifted students in, 65
    statistics on attendance at, 156
punishment, 99–100

Ravitch, Diane, 155
reading, 22–24, 161
Reagan, Ronald, 2

"Reason for School Dropouts, The"
(Royko), 121
records, 18–19
religion, 8
in schools, 87–88
remedial courses, 156
responsibility, 44–45, 93–94, 102–
103
Royko, Mike, 121

safety-related programs, 140, 152
school boards, 161
election of, 16, 157
powers and functions of, 15–17
of private schools, 16–17
School Book, The (Postman and
Wiengartner), 5
school districts, 15
allocation of funds by, 21
schools
academic standards of, 145
budgets of, 16, 18
desegregation of, 10, 155
educational achievements of,
155–158
educational goals of, 153–154
environment in, 119, 145, 162
evaluation by, 18, 62, 144
minority enrollment in, 39, 69,
155
overcrowding of, 10
student problems in, 117–127
traditional aims of, 157
see also elementary schools; high
schools; private schools
schools taxes, 4, 13–14
school year, 135, 136, 142–143, 161
science, 3, 18, 29–30, 145, 161
self-image, 71–80
parental contribution to, 72–78,
91–92
sexual stereotyping and, 78–80
senior citizens, 14
sex education, 111–114, 140, 152,
159
sexual roles
career choices and, 37, 79–80
stereotyping of, 37, 38, 54, 78–80

siblings, 8, 48, 102–103
Sizer, Theodore R., 124
sleep, 9, 11
social studies, 31–33, 145
social welfare agencies, 138
special education, 61–63
special programs, 58–69, 156–157
stress, 130–134
students
behavior problems in, 95–110,
117–134
development of character traits
in, 3, 13, 89–90, 154
dreams of, 43
instilling excellence in, 3, 160
learning capacity of, 147
rights of, 20, 58, 61, 63, 68, 80
see also gifted children; parent-
child relationship; troubled
students
study skills, 3, 6–7, 13, 50–52
substance abuse, 10, 127–130
prevention of, 128–129, 140, 152
statistics on, 127
treatment of, 129–130
warning signs of, 129
success, 91–94
parental guidance and, 91–92,
125
suicide, 133–134
survival skills, 158
suspension, 20

teachers
administrative functions of, 135,
138
ideal qualities of, 10–11, 119–120
salaries of, 10
school problems perceived by, 9–
10
see also parent-teacher
relationship
teenage pregnancy, 39, 111, 112
television, 52–57
advantages of, 55
family rules for, 7, 48, 55–57, 121
statistics on student viewing of,
53

values conveyed by, 52–53, 54–55, 111, 114
tests, 141
  preparing for, 51
  records of, 19
  student evaluation, 62, 63
time-on-task, 135–150
  definition of, 135
  in elementary schools, 136–137
  reasons for loss of, 139–142
  school year length and, 135, 136, 142–143
  strategies for improvement in, 142–147, 148–150
tough love, 130
troubled students, 117–134
  help for, 123–126, 129–130, 132–133
  warning signs of, 122–123, 129, 134
  see also stress; substance abuse; suicide

truancy, 122–123, 136
Universal Declaration of Human Rights, 5
values, 85–90, 154
  conflicts of, 86
  parental communication of, 88–90, 92–94
Van Buren, Abigail, 116
vocational education, 38–44
  basic academic courses in, 40
  follow-up support services of, 41
  hallmarks of quality in, 44
Vocational Education Act (VEA), 38
volunteers, 14–15
  student, 141–142
Weingartner, Charles, 5
work ethic, 43, 44–45, 93–94, 159
work habits, 3, 6–7, 13, 50–52
writing, 24–25, 161

THE PARENT POWER FOUNDATION

A Non-Profit Foundation

The Parent Power Foundation offers a variety of workshops, seminars, and train-the-trainer programs for parents, teachers, administrators, and interested individuals. These programs are designed to meet the needs of your school district, corporation, or organization. For further information write:

Lawrence E. Mazin, Ed.D.
The Parent Power Foundation
1010 West Orange Grove Road
Tucson, Arizona   85704